Richmond and Swaledale

Richmond and Swaledale

An illustrated visit to a beautiful dale

PETER MOPPETT

HAYLOFT

First published by Hayloft Publishing Ltd., 2017

A CIP catalogue record for this book is available from the British Library

ISBN 978-1-910237-32-8

Designed, printed and bound in the EU

Hayloft policy is to use papers that are natural, renewable and recyclable products and made from wood grown in sustainable forests. The logging and manufacturing processes are expected to conform to the environmental regulations of the country of origin.

Hayloft Publishing Ltd,
a company registered in England number 4802586
2 Staveley Mill Yard, Staveley, Kendal, LA8 9LR (registered office)
L'Ancien Presbytère, 21460 Corsaint, France (editorial office)

Email: books@hayloft.eu
Tel: 07971 352473
www.hayloft.eu

Frontispiece image: Painting of Richmond town beneath the Castle Keep

Contents

I would like to dedicate this book to the memory of the many lead miners and smelters of Swaledale, who so tragically and unknowingly put themselves in harm's way, (so many of them sadly cutting short their lives), while following their trade, in their quest for a better life for themselves and their families.

Introduction

Since my days at Catterick in the late 1950s, Swaledale, the most northern dale in the Yorkshire Dales National Park, has always been for me a wonderful area in which to roam and explore. But of course, it is not really a single dale, but two dis-similar twins, joined as it were at the hip, because Arkengarthdale leaves Swaledale at Reeth, rising rather ruggedly towards Sleightholme Moor and Tan Hill. The two dales have always had a close relationship, especially concerning their lead mining activities, in which the two dales' communities mixed readily with a common purpose.

Richmond, is a town with a very special relationship to Swaledale, in that, once the industrial interests became established, Richmond rapidly became the main administrative centre for all the dales' activities. I do not recall ever seeing a comprehensive guide book dealing specifically with Richmond and I therefore considered that it was time to produce one. However, given the special relationship between the town and Swaledale, it quickly became evident that the book's content should deal with the total subject matter, dealing with the social and economic development of both.

Before looking closely at either town or dale, perhaps we should examine how such a wonderfully varied and beautiful landscape came into being in the first place – remembering of course that the dale was not always as benign as its residents would have wished.

Peter Moppett, 2016.

1
The Geology of the Dales

Our planet has always been subject to periodic climate change since the formation of its atmosphere. Ice Ages have occurred repeatedly and evidence shows that three distinct and different Ice Ages have caused huge ice sheets, each many hundreds of metres in thickness, to advance and retreat in turn across Europe and the British Isles in the last 500,000 years.

Conditions leading to the last Ice Age began about 30,000 years ago and by the passing of the following 10,000 years, ice had advanced southward from the Arctic regions to cover almost all of the British Isles and Ireland; in the process, dropping adjacent sea levels by about 120 metres (400 feet). This exposed around twenty miles of existing sea bed around these islands.

By 16,000BC the ice advance had stabilised and thereafter it began retreating. The actual recovery of land areas was extremely slow, taking some 3,000 years of minor ice advances and retreats to expose the terrain up to the present Scottish border area. The sheer weight of ice capping the land, equal to several hundred tonnes

These pictures of present Norwegian glacial conditions give an impression of the enormous forces present from the weight of ice and the power of glacial melt-water, which together are able to transform landscapes.

per square metre, together with the inexorable, grinding downward creep of several glacier tongues from higher to lower ground levels, destroyed ancient landscapes entirely. New valleys and river patterns emerged with the eventual total retreat of the ice. Rock strewn wildernesses slowly began to be colonised by mosses and coarse, clumped grasses, followed by super hardy conifer, like juniper, plus birch and alder.

From evidence left behind, both geological and archaeological, especially from skeletal and tool remains, it can be shown that mankind evolved more rapidly during the period following the last Ice Age, than at any time before. It is certain that the Bronze and Iron Ages came about following the exposure of mineral deposits by the retreating ice. The Yorkshire Dales, as they are presented today, are the direct result of the last ice incursion and no dale demonstrates this better than Swaledale.

Remains of post glacial birch woodland with traces of oak, alder and sallow found in two metre thickness of peat on Hope Moor, West of Stang Road, (picture courtesy of Reeth Museum).

The picture above shows a ruined seventeenth century farmhouse known as Crackpot Hall, situated high above Keld in upper Swaledale, facing a valley through which the present-day River Swale flows towards Muker. The building was abandoned in the 1950s following severe damage caused by land slippage and subsidence.

The hill shown to the right of the picture is Kisdon. Prior to the last glaciation, the river flowed southwards from the upper dale area on the opposite (right hand) shoulder of Kisdon, towards what is now the village of Thwaite. Its course was changed due to the narrow valley through which it originally flowed, being choked by morain deposited by the last glacial action. The Swale valley here shows very clearly the typical character and contours of a glacially shaped valley.

Water from West Stonesdale enters the Swale above Keld. This side valley to Swaledale demonstrates a completely unspoilt character left by the last glacial period. It rises steeply to its summit, where it meets the Reeth to Kirkby Stephen road and the location of the Tan Hill Inn (the highest public house in the England).

A seam of shale, which surfaces at Tan Hill, was found in the thirteenth century to contain low grade coal, which was relatively easily mined from bell pits, worked by horse and rope lifts from the surface. Bell pits were so named as, in cross section, they were shaped like a church bell. Evidence of several pits can be seen quite easily and samples of coal can be picked up readily from remaining spoil heaps, especially from where burrowing animals have brought deposits to the surface.

The Tan Hill seam was worked in this way from at least 1384, when earliest records describing the coal mining operations were made, showing that coal was being supplied to Richmond Castle. The quality of the coal was poor, but mixed for burning with peat, it provided a good warmth and was easily kept going overnight and revived in the mornings. The coal is still used to this day by the owners of Tan Hill Inn for a warming fire in the public bar.

By the end of the seventeenth century, the surface and near surface deposits were exhausted and coal could only be won from deeper mines which were expensively dug and required additional drainage and manpower, with more complicated lifting arrangements to operate successfully. Tan Hill coal mixed with peat was also used in great quantities by the lead smelting and lime kiln operations throughout the Yorkshire Dales and nearby upper Eden Valley. In the seventeenth century, it was found that the low grade coal could be converted to a better quality, carbon-rich coke, which became known as cinders. The conversion took place in beehive shaped kilns and the resulting coke produced a far greater heat and became sought after for steam raising for engines powering industry and for iron making and general forge purposes, following the seventeenth century Industrial Revolution.

The Tan Hill Inn and, below, evidence of an early Bell-Pit mine.

The last organised coal mine at Tan Hill closed in 1929, just after the General Strike, due to better fuel being generally available at cheaper cost via modern transport from Yorkshire and Durham Collieries. Local people continued to work the upper seams of accessible coal at Tan Hill until the mid-1930s.

Tan Hill coal excavated by mining rabbits.

The Tan Hill Inn now stands alone at a height of 515 metres above sea level. Until they were demolished following the closure of the last organised mine, it was surrounded by a number of coal miner's cottages. The inn's use as a hostel continues following the closure, given the ongoing demand from local farmers, hikers and other frequent visitors arriving by car, motorbike and bus.

The geological development of the northern dales has left them particularly rich in mineral deposits like iron and lead. The lead ore galena, (lead sulphide), has been mined extensively in the area, certainly since the Roman invasion of Britain in the first century. Its availability has led to continual human occupation and development of the area in the time from then to the present day.

2
Richmond: Early History

Perched upon its rocky shelf above the unpredictable River Swale at the eastern end of Swaledale, Richmond must undoubtedly be ranked high among the most picturesque of North Yorkshire's market towns.

Its attractiveness is enhanced by its geography and by the way in which it evolved, growing over the years from its beginning as a Norman stronghold. One must be extremely fit to live in Richmond, as many of its streets are inclined at severe angles and a visit to its shopping centre for residents of Cravengate, Bargate, Cornforth Hill and Frenchgate, to name but a few streets, necessitates an energy sapping climb which, for many, must be a daunting prospect.

Ignoring the profusion of cars which daily invade its centre, the town has a permanent atmosphere of lasting charm in which one can discover so many unspoiled remnants of post Conquest English history. The town site has no positively known history before the Norman invasion. However, given the proliferation of Bronze and Iron Age sites throughout the length of Swaledale and in close proximity to Richmond; as at the important Celtic site of Stanwick, as well as the obvious strategic importance which the Romans gave to the area, indicated by the size and status of the excavated finds at the site of the Roman remains at Catterick Bridge, it is likely that the site occupied by the Norman fortress and township was equally valued and consistently used as a stronghold site by earlier people.

The existence of copper deposits beside the River Swale in Billy Banks, not far upstream from the town, which did not cease to be worked until 1912, would not have gone unnoticed by these earlier people and this would have been an added incentive for them to occupy the site. It is feasible that any Bronze Age or Celtic settlement, Saxon hamlet or township pre-existing on the site would have been entirely covered and obliterated by the Norman inspired building work which took place following the invasion of 1066.

A glance at English early history will show that the pre-conquest kingdom of Northumbria comprised the two earlier fiefdoms of Deira and Bernicia, together extending over territory from the Humber in the south to the Tweed in the north. Deira, the southern part of this kingdom, had been the fiefdom of the Saxon King Ribald Oswine, until he was murdered in 651AD on the instructions of Oswiu, the feudal lord of Bernicia. About 659 AD, a small monastery in which prayers were to be said for the murdered Oswine and those responsible for his death, was founded by King Oswiu at Gilling, a few miles north-east of present day Richmond, in order to expiate his sin in connection with their souls.

An early medieval brooch depicting scenes from the 'Harrowing of the North'. Picture courtesy of Richmond Museum.

By the time of the Norman Conquest, the Gilling onastery had fallen into ruin and Edwin, a Saxon Earl of the period, who had extensive lands in Yorkshire, had built a large hall on the site. In the year 1069, Yorkshire felt the brutal, iron hand of King William. A large Danish force had landed from their boats in the Humber and had been met and joined by an army of Scots and much of the northern Saxon nobility, (including Edwin), together with their men-at-arms, all hopeful of defeating the new king by their combined might.

William's Norman army marched north in force to meet the threat, and the combined Danes, Scots and Saxons were besieged at York. The siege took six long months to take the ultimate effect in starving out the beleaguered allies, during which time another force of Danes arrived and plundered Peterborough Cathedral. William permitted the Danish leader to keep the gold and other valuables stolen in the process and bribed with additional money from William, he left for Denmark with all his ships and the Danes from York. This left the surviving Saxons and their Scots allies at York, severely weakened and at the mercy of William. Edwin and his brother managed to escape, but were later killed by their own men.

William then ordered dreadful revenge upon the Saxon communities of the north in what became known as the 'Harrowing of the North'; laying waste the whole of the northern countryside. Contemporary accounts of the action speak of people and animals put to the sword, corpses left unburied, villages burned to the ground and widespread famine.

In recognition of his actions and bravery during the initial battles of the Conquest, and for his participation in the brutality with which William had decimated the northern area; also, as in his view someone trustworthy was needed to control the remaining northern population, William granted his nephew, Alain le Roux, (Alan Rufus 'The Red'), Earl of Britany: 'All towns and lands which lately belonged to Earl Edwin in Yorkshire, with all the Knights fees, churches and other privileges and customs in as free and honourable a manner as the same Edwin held them.' With this honour, Alan Rufus won estates in total, consisting of 440 manors throughout England, with a very large concentration in the north. So began, a ferociously oppressive, permanent occupation of the whole Yorkshire area.

Initially Earl Alan Rufus occupied the Gilling site of Edwin's residence but he decided the site was unsuitable, needing a more imposing and menacing Norman castle structure with which to better control the deprived, but surviving inhabitants of the shire, who were then living outside of the law and who, together with Scots raiders who were constantly on the rampage from the north, were an aggrevating cause for concern and were exceedingly dangerous. In 1071, he decided to remove his forces from Gilling, to the present fortress site above the River Swale and work began upon the construction of the castle. He named the newly selected site, 'Riche Monte' meaning rich or splendid hill. It and the town which grew around it, later became known as Richmond.

Alain le Roux receives the grant of lands, previously held by Edwin, Earl of Mercia, from his uncle Willam the Bastard, King of England, to whom he swears fealty. (Detail from a thirteenth century history, held by the British Library; Ref. MS Faust. B VII, fo.72v.).

He also, and at about the same time, builte a motte and bailey castle at Middleham, which was occupied, together with Norman soldiers, by his brother Ribald.

Above, Richmond Castle and town seen from River View, below left Castle well and right west wall detail.

The original castle structure took the form of a triangular, walled enclosure with a fortified single gate. Earl Rufus' formal accommodation was situated in the south east corner, centred around buildings on the edge of the rocky escarpment and known now as Scolland's Hall, (named after the Earl's steward). A gate beneath these buildings gave entry into an enclosed area known as The Cockpit, which overlooked the river valley below. Much of the original fortification can still be seen and noticeable in many places in the masonry is a herringbone

pattern method of construction, which was typical of Saxon masons' practice in England during the pre-conquest period. It is more than likely therefore, that Earl Rufus employed forced Saxon labour in many phases of the original construction work. Seventy-five years later, the castle underwent a major strengthening reconstruction with the addition of its Keep and the greatly improved barbican and entry gate.

Above, the Norman Keep,
right Scollands Hall
and below the Cockpit garden below
Scollands Hall.

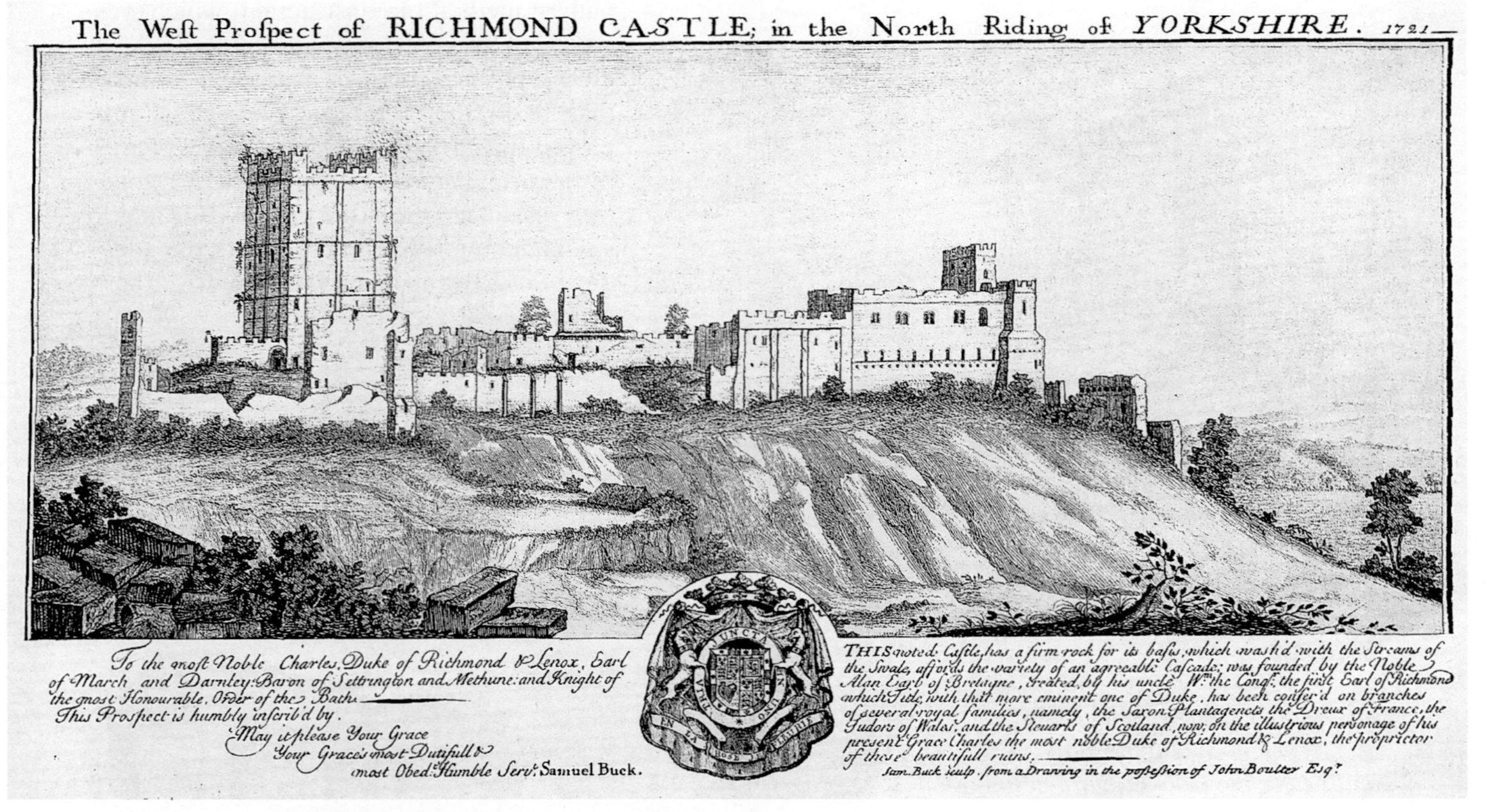

Above engraving courtesy of Richmond Museum and below The Foss in spate.

Legend suggests that King Arthur and his knights dwell in caverns deep beneath Richmond Castle, ready to rise in order to save England from future disaster. Another legend associated with the castle concerns a drummer boy of the Napoleonic War period, who was allegedly lowered into an underground passage discovered by his soldier comrades wishing to plunder Arthur's treasure. He was instructed to beat his drum while negotiating the length of the tunnel so that his comrades could follow the sound from the surface. The story says that the sound of his drum was followed for a distance of about half a mile towards Easby Abbey, before it could be heard no more and the poor boy was never seen again. An inscribed plaque marks the spot on the present foot-path to the abbey, where the sound of the drum was said to be last heard.

On its way past the town, the River Swale skirts the castle on two sides, forming a right angled bend, before tumbling over a very large stepped waterfall, known as The Foss. In doing so, the river adds significantly to the town and castle's positional strength. The river's catchment area extends upwards over the whole dale which carries its name, as well as its numerous side valleys. Sudden upstream rainstorms can cause alarmingly rapid rises in water levels, sometimes resulting in a noticeable 'bore', which can travel downstream at considerable speed. The river is renowned as being somewhat unpredictable and dangerous to the unwary.

3
The Town and Trade

As can easily be seen from existing evidence, the town was established co-incidental with the castle's construction and was largely contained within the overall stronghold. It became a formidable fortification and was considerably added to over the following hundred years or so in both construction and status.

Although the castle and its curtain walls were built of stone, (the castle was the first British Norman castle to be entirely stone built), the original wall enclosing the town was constructed of an earth and rubble foundation with a wooden palisade fence. Three 'Bars', (main entrance gates) were constructed; Frenchgate, Finkle Street, and Briggate. The Frenchgate and Finkle Street gateways were demolished in 1773, in order to permit wider passage for horse and ox drawn wagons.

Friars Wynd, left, and Briggate, above.

Briggate, situated on what is now Cornforth Hill, leading down to Bridge Street was only wide enough to permit the passage of pedestrians and packhorses, but the later road improvements within the town diverted larger traffic to other routes and this gateway was subequently left intact.

There were other, smaller exits from the town, as shown by the present small gateway in Friars Wynd, which carries a notice advising that it was used by townspeople fetching water from a spring near the Friarage. This gate and the Briggate, reached via the narrow passageway known as The Barr, are the only

Richmond market place, the largest in the country, has at its centre, the Church of the Holy Trinity. The traditional market cross, takes the form of a stone obelisk, created in 1771, to replace an original which covered a large water cistern, built to supply water to various parts of the town.

entrances through the original town wall which have survived.

Given the safety afforded by the stronghold, the town very quickly attracted a sizeable population, becoming a centre for trade and commerce. In 1145 the Earl of Richmond, conferred certain rights upon the 'Burgesses of Richmond', which opened the way for them to trade within the confines of the town. This act on his part was perhaps the first anywhere in England to institute a form of municipal corporation for a town.

These rights were confirmed in 1268 by John, Earl of Richmond, when the first specific mention was made in the Grant of Rights to markets and fairs. They were confirmed again on 30 June 1328, this time in a Charter granted by King Edward III and by these means, Richmond became a centre for trade and commerce, trading typically in wool, grain (wheat for bread, barley for brewing ale), iron, lead, livestock, butchered meat, fish, hides and tallow, vegetables, dairy produce and cloth; as well as pottery and assorted implements.

In 1278, Edward I granted the Earl of Richmond a Royal Charter; to the effect that he and his heirs should have for ever at his Manor of Richmond a fair every Year, to continue for four days: 'on the vigil day and morrow of the Exaltation of the Holy Cross and for one day following.' These four days centre around the 14 September each year.

Medieval fairs were great occasions in the town's annual calendar. They attracted English and foreign merchants, eager to purchase the local wool, lead, hides and other commodities; as well as itinerant traders, travelling entertainers, fortune tellers and others from far and wide. People of the town and surrounding villages, not able to travel far beyond their homes, were given the rare opportunity of meeting old friends and hearing news first hand from afar.

The fairs were also an occasion to hold periodic courts of law in which public grievances could be heard and civil offenders punished. Above all, they added to the monetary wealth and general prosperity of the town. An additional fair, held on Palm Sunday evening in each year, was granted to Richmond in 1576 by Queen Elizabeth I. This same charter granted the town a market every Saturday; and a fair or market on the Saturday, once each fortnight between Palm Sunday Eve and the Feast of the Holy Nativity, together with all other markets or fairs which they before had or held.

The earlier grants and charters channelled considerable income to the King; to the Earl; to the burgesses and also to the traders of goods who were attracted to the many opportunities which were afforded them by the fair and the periodic markets; but the fabric of the town in general, especially its defences, were apparently not

Part of the original Richmond town wall.

The Holy Trinity Church – the 12th century church standing proudly in the Market square, belonged in the Middle Ages to the very powerful Abbey of St Mary at York. After the General Dissolution action by King Henry 8th, it was acquired by the town Burgesses and was secularised with shops and trading stalls built in and around it. It houses the "Curfew" Bell, which was rung every day at 8PM, a practice, which common tradition says, dates back to Rufus the Red's command, to better control the town's inhabitants, given the unrest existing following the "Harrying of the North". It was also known as "The Passing Bell", rung on occasions of death of a town resident; Nine for an adult male; Six for a woman; and three for a child.

considered at that time, when spending any sizeable part of this income.

Since the time of King Stephen in 1135, affluent Richmond and its surrounding countryside had been a continuing target for groups of marauding Scots, intent on pillage, murder and rape – which were equally practised by the English against the Scots in a time of Border warfare. Bands of ferocious brigands were difficult to fight off and could only be repulsed at great cost, both financial and human. The town had often attempted to buy them off, paying the raiders not to put the shire to fire and sword. Contemporary reports complain of the Scots leaders taking such payments and turning a blind eye to the continuing carnage committed by their raiding parties.

In the early fourteenth century the town's outer defences must have been deemed entirely unsuitable to ward off the Scottish raiders, as on 25 February 1312, King Edward II granted the Earl of Richmond liberty to surround the town with a stone wall. The construction work of that time was either very slow or sub-standard, because only thirteen years later in 1325, the town walls were deemed to be in such a state of dilapidation that they required extensive, urgent and costly work in order to bring them to a standard suitable for the town's protection.

At this time, King Edward II gave John, Earl of Richmond a 'grant of murage', enabling him to levy tolls on all goods brought to and sold at the town market, in order to pay for the erection of the town wall. This grant was valid for five years, during which time the wall appears to have been completed. As sometimes happens in modern times, adequate municipal maintenance appears not to have been carried out properly, or at all in ensuing years, as on 14 May 1399, King Henry IV granted a further murage on the town in order to repair the wall, which was again, 'very ruinous and in need of reparation.'

The town's unrivalled prosperity was not to last indefinitely. Other towns which had grown in the region, attracted by the example set by Richmond, sought, and were similarly granted by succeeding kings of England, rights to hold annual fairs and periodic markets. Towns such as Middleham, Bedale, Masham, Staindrop and Barnard Castle all vied with Richmond and each other to attract trade and the resulting cash flow. This financial rivalry between Richmond and its neighbouring towns continued throughout the centuries.

In the mid-seventeenth century, during the time of the Commonwealth, a statement was drawn up by Richmond for submission to Parliament, describing how much Richmond would be unfairly affected if fortnightly fairs were to be granted to Middleham. It read, '...That the town of Richmond and country thereabouts consisted much in the trade of knitted stockings and that a place so near as Middleham and situated in the Dales with the people of which the trade and commerce of Richmond did very much consist, would drain in short time the greatest part of that trade to it to the utter ruin of families in Richmond.' The statement went on to complain that, ' thirteen companies of tradesmen and 300 masters of families, having little subsistence besides their trade from the neighbouring people, that its fairs and markets cannot but suffer deeply if their resources be taken.'

The practice of knitting stockings seems to have extended back to about 1560, when Queen Elizabeth I was said to have favoured wearing woollen hose of the kind produced in Richmond and so began a fashion. Richmond had apprentice schemes in place for orphans of the poorhouse, with prescribed, albeit meagre, conditions of food and board for the luckless apprentices. Knitting in Swaledale and other dales areas continued in large measure until recent times, especially within the farming and mining communities, where the product realised a much needed additional income in time of hardship.

The competition brought about by other town fairs and markets in the early fifteenth century caused such significant falls in annual income to Richmond that, as a result of their 'scarcely being able to raise a quarter' of the £40 annual sum required by the King according to charter, the burgesses at one time petitioned King Henry VI, requesting that they be relieved of the duty to pay him the sum required in that year. The King graciously responded by reducing the sum to a level of £12. Notwithstanding these drawbacks, Richmond's prosperity continued to attract, bringing about the need for additional housing, rudimentary hospitals and sanitation, and above all, water supplies, which in medieval times were tenuous in the extreme; dependent upon the weather; and at best, the water was discoloured and muddy; at worst, filthy and a distinct risk to health.

By the middle of the twelfth century, the town's population had grown considerably. There were chapels within the castle, but these could not accommodate the numbers of townspeople requiring to make their devotions. Two churches were built at that time, one in the Market Square dedicated to The Holy Trinity; the other, built outside the town walls, dedicated to the Virgin Mary and destined to become the parish church in later years. In dire need of attention after 200 years use, Holy Trinity was re-built in 1360 and was in use until Henry VIII's General Dissolution, when it appears to have been once again in a state of bad dilapidation. Its south aisle had been demolished and a decision was taken not to continue using the whole church, which remained in a ruinous state for another 200 years.

A part of it did remain in some use however, as it is recorded that some form of service took place within its walls up to 1712. In 1740, the town corporation leased part of it to tradesmen for building several shops, one of which was built into the base of the tower. Four years later, the corporation refurbished its much reduced nave area and common services were again resumed. From 1753, celebration of the Holy Sacraments was forbidden within the refurbished church. Dire penalties were prescribed for anyone celebrating marriage within the church, which included a term of fourteen years' transportation. The church has been in secular use since 1973 and now houses the Green Howards Museum.

Plague

Contact with the outside world afforded by the fairs aided prosperity, but also brought with it the severe risks of the time. The town and surrounding countryside suffered from repeated visits from plague, which, with each outbreak, significantly reduced the population. Risk of plague surfacing again was ever present following an

The Black Friars tending to those sick with the plague.

initial outbreak which reached Yorkshire from the south in 1349. It recurred wherever circumstances of squalid and insanitary living conditions existed. Epidemics often followed periods of crop failure and famine, which were not uncommon, given the frequency at which exhausted and infertile land was expected to produce harvests with little husbandry beyond crop rotation.

Inhabitants of townships and villages, already brought low by a starvation diet, soon succumbed to the ravages of infection, to the extent of some villages being entirely wiped-out, never to be populated again. In 1349 and 1362, the Black Death came to Richmond, killing some 20 per cent of the population at large, as well as about a third of the clergy, who would have been attempting to minister to the sick at the time. These events were followed by further epidemic outbreaks in 1369, and again in 1374. Whether they were actually caused by bubonic plague, influenza, typhus, smallpox or cholera, they caused a drastic effect upon the economy of Yorkshire in general and Swaledale particularly took a long time to recover.

Doctors of the time tried in vain to stem the epidemics with their limited skills and medicines, but they also found themselves forced by law to acquiesce to the clergy, who had prior rights and expectations with respect to the sick and who, instead of treating the body of the patient, exercised the right to first treat his or her soul. Few parish priests willingly undertook such dangerous duties however. Instead it often fell to monks of the nearest order, in whom the highest infection and mortality rates were encountered. So much so, that following plague outbreaks, the various dioceses were forced to effect widespread recruiting to make up for the huge numbers of monks lost.

During excavation work which took place during the construction of the Richmond railway, immense quantities of human bones were found in the vicinity of St Martin's Priory, in what were possibly plague pits from one or other of the epidemics. After the plague outbreak of 1349, with much arable land left unploughed; with few ploughmen left alive to till it and the surviving villain class in open revolt against law and custom, landowners began substituting sheep pasture for arable land.

King Edward III brought Flemish weavers to England in order to expand the limited skills of the general population in weaving woollen cloth, resulting very quickly in the demand and costs for wool being dramatically

Arkengarthdale

increased. Nowhere was the increase in the wool trade used to financial advantage more than in Richmond and Swaledale, where the sparse and hither-to, difficult to farm hill land was turned over to sheep.

Despite laws, such as the Statute of Labourers, which was passed in 1351, attempting to restrict wage demands, the common man's life changed for the better following the plague outbreak of 1348/49. Farm labourers, hitherto restricted by law from moving far from their home village, began to migrate to where they could command better wages and living. Due to the drastically reduced level of population, workmen and servants for the merchant classes were in demand and prosperous towns like Richmond were like magnets, quickly attracting replacement labour to restore its losses. Its trade restored, all the more profitable due to the increase in the wool trade, the town went from strength to strength.

Richmondshire was to suffer a further massive depopulation from epidemic at the end of the sixteenth century. Beginning in August 1597, illness swept northwards through communities, taking its toll of lives. The epidemic abated somewhat during the winter months, but returned with great violence in the spring of 1598. Although exact records are unclear, sufficient clarity exists to suggest that some 3,000 persons in the area died as a result of the year's advance of the infection.

Upstream from Richmond, the Swale valleys are now an area of dales hill farming and tourism, but until the beginning of the twentieth century, the area was also intensively mined to extract and smelt its extensive lead deposits. Lead has been mined in the area from the time of the early Roman occupation, as indicated by an ingot, or 'pig' of smelted lead inscribed 'Hadrian', found adjacent to an early mine near the village of Marrick in Swaledale.

Swaledale's early lead mines were concentrated mainly in Arkengarthdale and in the area around the present village of Grinton, but as mining expertise improved and as deposits of galena ore were found higher up in the dale and its side valleys, lead mining activity increased in scale to cover almost all of the Swale catchment area by the end of the sixteenth century. A single mine in later years, cutting good seams of ore, could produce 2,000 pigs of lead per year. Dales lead passed through Richmond from medieval times up to the demise of the mines, generating an extremely healthy level of income for Richmond and its merchants.

Records show that in 1325, at the time when tolls in aid of funds for the rebuilding of the Richmond town walls were being levied upon goods sold in Richmond market, the typical toll rate for a single cartload of lead was charged at two pence, (approximately £6.50 at current valuation). It is also known from medieval records, that 700 tons of Swaledale lead for the roofs of Waltham and Clairvaux Abbeys was shipped from Yarm and Boroughbridge to London and France between 1179 and 1183, on orders from King Henry II. Lead was brought from the dale on the backs of specially bred ponies called Jaggers. They were small, compact and very strong, able to carry two pigs of lead, each weighing about one and a half hundredweight in wicker panniers.

Up to the closure of the workings, the townspeople of Richmond would have been well used to the sight of teams of packhorses laden with pigs of lead being brought into Richmond for sale and onward transit by cart and packhorse towards the river Tees at Yarm via Scorton, or the River Ure at Boroughbridge, being the nearest navigable rivers with access to the sea. However, cart and packhorse transport was slow, difficult and costly, especially given the condition of the green trackways and few established roadways existing at the time.

Richmond Station

Almost the only surfaced road available for the purpose towards the end of the eighteenth century was the old Roman road south from Catterick to Boroughbridge and over the passage of centuries this had become extremely difficult to negotiate. Merchants became desperate to find means of reliably transferring weighty and bulky materials to the available ports; this included not only lead, but wool, slate, limestone and lime for the furnaces of Cleveland; all of which were important sources of income for Richmond and Swaledale. The gradients of the Swale were considered to be too great and its nature too turbulent for it to be made navigable as far as Richmond (although a measure using a system of flood dams was considered), but the available roads were at most times impossible to negotiate, especially in winter. It was time for urgent remedial measures, notwithstanding their cost, and schemes were sought to overcome the problems.

In 1765, when most of the country was rushing to follow the example of the Duke of Bridgewater's canal venture serving his Worsley mines, a group including persons of influence in Richmond, obtained an Act of Parliament, which permitted works to take place, enabling the Swale to be made navigable as far upstream as Morton. The scheme was to include the Bedale Beck and the Codbeck to be canalised from their confluences with the Swale, up to Bedale and Thirsk respectively. Work was actually started on this scheme, but was not taken far before failing through legal difficulties and lack of funding. The existing section of canal at Bedale, near the railway station was actually part of this aborted scheme.

Above, Richmond Railway Station Cottages and below, model of station, on display at and courtesy of Richmond Museum.

Mercury Bridge.

Another scheme was envisaged in 1800, when a privately funded survey was made which projected another canal, 70 miles long in total. It was to have run from Boroughbridge to Piercebridge, with navigable arms to the River Tees at Worsall and to Richmond and Bedale. Its projected cost was estimated as £107,000, against a perceived income at the time of £15,000 per annum. This scheme did not get off the ground and was probably overtaken by events of 25 years later with the coming of another rush, this time to build railways.

In 1846, the Darlington to Richmond Railway Company opened its line to Richmond's riverside station and the cost of transporting Swaledale lead to the quayside was reduced by more than one third, to two shillings and ten pence per ton and transported it much more quickly. As well as freight services, the railway operated four passenger services each way daily, (with two on Sundays).

It necessitated the building of a new road, descending from Frenchgate, crossing the River Swale by means of a bridge, in order to provide a route from the town market area to the station yard. The bridge was later to be named 'Mercury' Bridge, in honour of the Royal Corps of Signals, whose training establishment, at that time, was permanently stationed at Catterick Garrison. During the 1914/18 conflict with Germany, the road was extended from the station to serve Catterick Garrison as a link to the railway, using some of the 5,000 German Prisoners of War employed there on camp construction and road building.

With a later rail link serving it, joining the railway to Darlington at Catterick Bridge, the siting and construction of Catterick Garrison commenced in 1916. The garrison has existed in harmony with the town since that time, each drawing benefit from the other. Many thousands of regular soldiers and National Servicemen (including the author in 1958), travelling from all parts of the country to commence their service training at Catterick, experienced their first taste of military discipline on arrival at the yard of Richmond Station.

Although the railway, as a victim of the 1950s rail closures has been dismantled, the station building, together

The old railway track is now a bridleway, much enjoyed by walkers.

with the original railway cottages beside the old trackway, still stand and are a totally unspoiled example of Victorian railway charm. The station has been sympathetically renovated and given new life as a centre and community venue for meetings and exhibitions by local artists. It houses a cinema, a thriving cafeteria, and is further occupied by a variety of local entrepreneurs and independent businesses.

Lead mining in Swaledale had declined drastically by the end of the nineteenth century, as the available ore deposits became exhausted, or mining levels became too wet to work without costly pumping operations. Also, co-incidentally at that time, cheaper lead was being imported from abroad and Dales folk generally, men and women, were reduced to eking out a living from farming and their knitting skills.

Richmond's prosperity however continued with a whole range of commercial activity powered from earlier times by the important Swale River. It provided water energy at different times for: tanneries, dye works, water mills for flour and oats, a fulling mill, breweries, fish curing, warehouses, a paper mill, a copper mine, sawmills; and an early form of gasworks, which was the first of its kind in Europe, sited below the castle and operated by The Richmond Gas Light Company.

Other commercial activities developed in Richmond were: stabling, chandlery, and the extremely valuable and important wool processing operations of spinning and weaving

Opposite, the picturesque Swale at Easby Rail Bridge and the rail bridge over the River Swale at Easby.

The Mill House, Easby Abbey.

Above, River Swale, autumn colours at Easby and below, Caleb Readshaw.

The early postcard picture, opposite, probably dates from the mid-1920s, and shows a heavily overgrown castle. The original Richmond Gas works can be seen beside the river below the castle. Note also the modern barracks, built against the west wall of the castle area.

Foremost in the development of the early eighteenth century wool trade in Richmond was Caleb Readshaw, a prosperous wool merchant and draper. An old boy of Richmond School and town mayor, he saw and exploited an opportunity in the needs of the Dales mining communities to earn extra money in order to supplement their incomes from mining and the poor farming land of the Dales. Buying fleeces at comparatively low cost, he issued spun woollen yarn to mining families and others so they could knit a range of woollen goods such as, gloves, caps, mufflers and stockings. Exporting the finished products abroad, mainly to the Low Countries, he made huge profits in the process. He was additionally financially involved in lead mining operations throughout the Dales.

His imposing house, standing apart from the town, facing south, to the sun and the river and built, uncommonly for the time, in red brick, broadcast in uncertain terms, his wealth, in-

Caleb Readshaw's house in Richmond.

fluence and standing in eighteenth century Richmond.

By charter granted by Elizabeth I, Richmond had the privilege of sending two MPs to Parliament. The only persons permitted to vote for MP nominations were the occupiers of burgage houses (those with tenure of land for an annual rent). There were only 273 such persons in Richmond when, in 1760, Lawrence Dundas of Aske acquired 161 of these properties, thereby consolidating the nomination of Richmond Members of Parliament into his hands only. As a result, Richmond became known as a Pocket Borough.

4
Religious Influences

Saint Martin's Priory

Over the centuries, the Swale Valley has been the home of several religious orders, some of them dating from before the Conquest. Mainly as a result of the General Dissolution of Henry VIII, all have now gone from the scene. Some have left no trace beyond the briefest of reference, a shadow in some medieval record. Others, like the houses at Marrick and Ellerton have left a few tell-tale remnants of masonry above ground to offer witness to their one-time thriving existence, but houses like Easby, Greyfriars and St Martin's Priory have left behind impressive ruins to illustrate their importance and undoubted influence upon the town.

Given its strategic importance; its wealth and influence, as well as its early political and geographical position, it is little wonder that Richmond attracted so many religious orders and adherents to settle within, or in the immediate vicinity of the town walls.

Saint Martin's Priory.

The earliest religious house, of which there is any clear record, appears to be the Priory of St Martin, situated on the opposite bank of the Swale from the castle. What little remains of its buildings can be seen from the road to Catterick Garrison and from the old railway track, which is now a public bridleway.

St Martin's Benedictine Priory was founded in 1100. Although due to raiders and plague its numbers varied over the years of its existence, it housed a prior and ten monks nominally and was quite richly endowed for the time. Its adjacent land holdings amounted to over one hundred acres, but it had other lands in the area from which it derived income.

At the time of the General Dissolution in 1539, the priory had an annual income of a little over £45 (over £20,000 in today's money) plus what tithes in goods and produce it commanded. It operated its own corn mill on the adjacent bank of the Swale (now lost beneath the railway buildings) and would have had its own fishing facilities on the adjacent river bank, as well as ponds in which to keep a ready stock of fish taken from the river.

The ruins of St Martin's Priory as seen from the old railway track

The monks had a close relationship with the town and probably moved between it and the priory by fording the Swale in low water conditions, to walk up the lane skirting the town wall that is now Park Wynd.

It is thought that the monks from St Martin's Priory administered the early hospital dedicated to St Nicholas, which was situated overlooking the Swale Valley, at the top of Frenchgate, at the junction with Gallowgate and Maison Dieu, well apart from the town. The hospital was essentially established for the relief of the poor, sick and infirm people of the town, but it also administered lodging and refreshment of the most basic kind to travellers.

In the Pipe Roll of 1172, in the reign of Henry II, Ralph de Glanville is recorded to have bequeathed an annual sum of money equal to five seams of bread corn (ten shillings approximately), for the sick of the St Nicholas Hospital. In 1399, Henry IV granted patronage of the hospital to Ralph, Earl of Westmorland and in 1446, it was given by Henry VI to John, Duke of Bedford. It is mentioned in records of 1448, when it was repaired and refurbished following what was reported as advanced decay. (A timely event, considering the outbreak of the Black Death in the following year). It was endowed with its own gardens, orchard and arable lands.

In the fifteenth century, the prior of St Martin's was responsible for an annual sum of 21 shillings to be given, in providing for an anchoress dwelling on Maison Dieu. Anchorites were religious recluses, often walled into their living quarters with no direct contact with the outside world, beyond being fed daily by others through a hole in their confining wall.

Easby Abbey
About a mile downstream from the castle, reached today either by a lane leading from the B6271 road, or by footpaths from St Mary's Church or the old railway station; the ruins of Easby Abbey, and the still intact and used adjacent little church, stand beside the River Swale. Dedicated to St Agatha, and founded in 1152 by an order of Premonstratensian (White) Canons, the abbey prospered with a fairly relaxed, but austere lifestyle.

Easby Abbey and Saint Agatha's Church

The abbey was endowed with several highly productive parcels of prime agricultural land, a dovecote, a mill with a plentiful and constant supply of water with which to power it, as well as to brew their ale, and plenty of fish from the adjacent river. Attracted by its obvious wealth and relatively unprotected in its isolation from the town, the abbey suffered at the hands of raiding Scots on a few occasions. In 1346, when King David II of Scotland crossed the border, to be met and defeated by the English at the Battle of Neville's Cross near Durham City, the abbot of St Agatha's naively invited the English army to occupy billets on the abbey grounds. He was not prepared for what subsequently happened, as the English soldiers went on the rampage, causing more damage and desecration of the abbey than had occurred in any Scottish raid before.

Despite the abbot's appeals to King Edward III for reparations, the king was far too absorbed in his several wars to bother with pleas for money from a comparatively wealthy establishment such as Easby and the abbot was left to lick his wounds, making what he could from the situation.

The abbey was far from poor for the time. In 1538, it had a cash income in excess of £188 per year, (near £86,000 today), in addition to its many other tithed assets. In 1539, it too was suppressed on the order of King Henry VIII, as part of the General Dissolution. With the abbey disbanded, the buildings (with the exception of the little church of St Agatha standing adjacent to it), robbed of roofs, floors and much of their stonework, fell into complete ruin, leaving the present sad but romantic scene as a testament to its former glory. Its mill, on the adjacent bank of the Swale, was later renovated and modified as a dwelling.

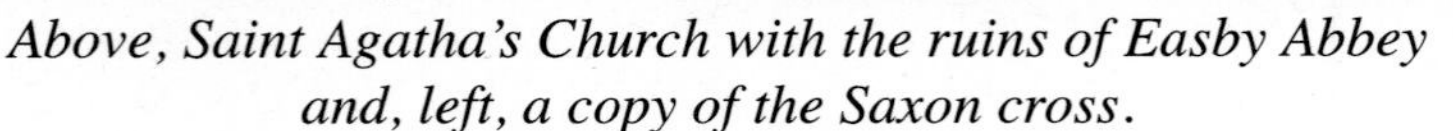

Above, Saint Agatha's Church with the ruins of Easby Abbey and, left, a copy of the Saxon cross.

Standing beside the ruins, St Agatha's Church pre-dates Easby Abbey by a considerable number of years and has obviously undergone a number of re-building and refurbishment operations in its history. It is mentioned in an ecclesiastical report of 1424, when it was re-dedicated, possibly after having been refurbished on that occasion.

In the process of later maintenance, fragments of an early seventh or eighth century Saxon cross, thought to have originated within the original church boundary, were discovered built into its walls, offering some evidence of the church's true age. The original fragments were given to the Victoria and Albert Museum, but copies were made which, reassembled, stand within the church. There are also some very fine examples of twelfth century wall paintings to be seen adorning the interior walls of the church. Their colours and the message they portray, remain almost as vivid as when they were painted, despite the passage of so many years.

Medieval wall paintings inside Saint Agatha's Church .

Greyfriars

Greyfriars tower, the bell tower of the Franciscan Friary which stood on the site until the General Dissolution, is one of the most distinctive monuments in the town. Standing, as it does, in the well-kept Friarage Gardens, it adds a touch of mystery and romance to the colourful display of flowers evident each summer within the peaceful surroundings of the little park.

The friary was founded in the middle of the thirteenth century by a group of monks who followed the extremely strict disciplines of life and prayer set up by St Francis of Assisi before his death in 1226. Under his rules, wearing a grey habit with a cowl and cloak, a Franciscan monk repudiated all property and devoted his life as a mendicant to prayer and the care of the poor and sick. At the time of the General Dissolution, the friary accommodated a prior and a total of twelve monks.

Given the beautiful construction of the ruined building left standing, the Franciscans were obviously held in high esteem by the influential and rich of the medieval town and surrounding area. They also took on the role of teachers and were often employed in matters of trust, such as the making of wills and testaments, as well as acting as arbiter in matters of dispute.

A small nunnery was built, which was sited adjacent to the friary and which housed a few Franciscan nuns known as Poor Clares. These nuns followed a regime similar to that of their mendicant neighbours, but if anything, the discipline under which they lived was even more strict. Both houses were closed by order of the General Dissolution and the buildings were afterwards subjected to the most abject destruction.

The site is now appropriately occupied by the Friary Hospital. The few Greyfriars' houses founded in mediaeval Britain were all built within, or as close as possible, to the host township in order to facilitate the mendicant life of the order (begging for alms and general sustenance would have been extremely difficult if friaries

Above, painting of Greyfriars tower, the bell tower of the Franciscan Friary and below, the Friary Hospital

had been sited elsewhere). All were obliterated as a result of the General Dissolution. The valuable stonework was generally quickly taken and used for other building purposes in town development. The remains at Richmond are unique, insofar that so much still remains above ground of the original friary structure and excavations on the site have revealed extensive remains of foundation stonework still existing beneath the surface.

Education

From their initial foundation, each religious order had its own arrangements for the education of novices, young men and boys, sent to live with the monks in order to learn and take up the ways of religious life. As part of their learning, they were taught to read and write and were given an understanding of mathematics and music, especially singing. In medieval times, teachers were permitted to teach only by diocesan authority. The prior of each establishment maintained close contact with his and other diocesan bishops and the best teachers were often moved to take positions with other establishments, causing a cross-fertilisation of practice and ideals. Teaching slowly began to assume importance within the church and established schools and universities began to be founded throughout the country, offering secular education. Schools generally did not begin to break away from church authority to become 'grammar' schools until after the Dissolution.

The site of the original grammar school in St Mary's Church yard,

Some form of school existed at Richmond as early as the first half of the fourteenth century. There is evidence dating from the mid-sixteenth century to indicate the existence of a grammar school, but its legitimacy is not clear. In 1544, in order to appease Queen Elizabeth I in the matter of the town burgesses' previous seizure of some valuable ecclesiastically owned land, the burgesses petitioned the Queen to grant permission for a free grammar school to be built with income from the land in question.

The Queen gave her consent to the petition on 14 March 1567, and the school was constructed in the grounds of the Parish Church of St Mary. The building lasted until 1677, when it was replaced by another small building in the churchyard. The school was enlarged to cater for expanding numbers in 1815 and lasted in use in the churchyard until 1850. The building was finally demolished in 1856, after having been derelict for six years.

The first buildings of the present school were opened in 1850 on a site opposite St Mary's Parish Church and have been extensively enlarged to cater for greater numbers of scholars in attendance from a catchment area which now extends far wider than the town area of Richmond. The school now forms part of a comprehensive school complex as a Sixth Form College.

Richmond School's Old Boys include: Charles Lutwidge Dodson (Lewis Carrol), who wrote the *Alice in Wonderland* books; Dr John Bathurst (Oliver Cromwell's physician); and many other notables.

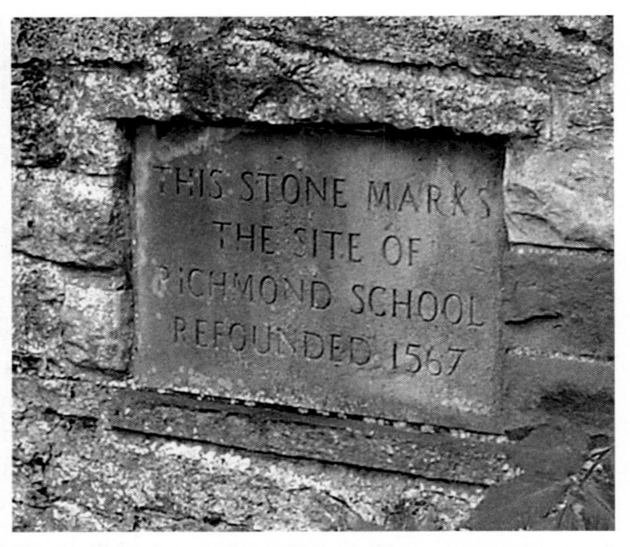

The commemorative stone marking the site of the original grammar school in St Mary's Church yard,

5
The Modern Town

A map of 1610 shows that Richmond was still in the main confined within its town walls, retaining the medieval pattern of houses bordering the Market Square, with a rear burgess or garden, extending outward to the line of the town wall. Examples of these can be clearly seen today in the area of Park Wynd. Houses external to the town walls were mainly confined to linear developments bordering the main streets into the town, like Frenchgate, Bargate and Newbiggin, or were isolated mills, farms and the like, well away from the town.

In the fourteenth and early fifteenth centuries, Richmond's trade seriously declined, principally as a result of two major devastating influences. Firstly, the continual Scottish raids following the Battle of Bannockburn, when the Scots won a decisive victory, decimating the English Army and killing or capturing for ransom much of the English nobility. An Inquest report of 1339, found Richmond and its castle to be greatly dilapidated and destroyed, due to the ferocity of repeated attacks by Border raiders. Secondly, repeated epidemics, which had decimated the population.

The present day Richmond Georgian Theatre Royal.

From top: the Georgian Theatre Royal stage area, the stalls and the stage wings.

Much of the town's wealth had gone to pay off the Scots in 1316 and again in 1322 and the town's markets had become less and less attractive to traders, who had many other, safer market towns to choose from in which to pursue their trade. From the time of the General Dissolution and the Reformation, when the Church's influence in secular matters began to wane, the burgesses, (the town council of the day), began to take greater control and influence over municipal affairs. Trade in Richmond began to improve as a direct result of their influence. The thirteen trade guilds, from which most if not all of the burgesses came, managed the interests of the town as well as those of their particular trades, often coincidentally.

Richmond's renewed prosperity attracted many more people to the town. The incoming population found work for wages in most of the trades and their success attracted others in growing numbers. The town began a marked growth outward in the late seventeenth century. Poorer areas, such as Maison Dieu, which is recorded at the time as being an area of filthy hovels, with most of the long established medieval houses, were gradually overbuilt with better housing. Additional suburb areas were created, where new supplies of water could be found. Open sewers were replaced with better, underground drainage (albeit, still draining into the river) and proper, regular arrangements were made to deal with the filth littering the streets, emanating from the many transport and haulage animals entering and leaving the town daily, as well as from the animals brought into the markets for onward sale.

Above the Georgian Theatre Royal dressing room and right, the stage lifting mechanism.

Above, Newbiggin and below, Newbiggin Square, previously a cattle market and public execution area. Pictured right, Market Square (above) and St. Mary's Church and Maison Dieu (below), both views seen from the keep of Richmond Castle.

By the eighteenth century, as lead production began to peak and the wool trade expanded to become Richmond's money spinner, outer areas of the town such as Newbiggin, previously a cattle market and execution ground, were being redeveloped in the open, tree-lined Georgian style. The town began to take on a distinct Georgian appearance generally, with old buildings demolished and rebuilt, or simply refurbished in the new styles. Richmond became an attractive venue for trade and entertainment and the attraction brought with it increasing numbers of visiting traders and purchasers. These required food and accommodation, which led to enlarged and increasing numbers of hotels and taverns.

Many visiting traders decided that Richmond was the place to live permanently, causing more permanent shops to be established in the Market Square; some, abutting and intruding into Holy Trinity Chapel. The town's increasing success required better means of communication and facilities, resulting in improved road systems. A racecourse was introduced at the top of Gallowgate and in 1788, a small theatre was opened, which still exists, sited opposite Greyfriars, beside the entrance to Friars Wynd.

The threatre became Richmond's Theatre Royal, the most authentic and complete eighteenth century Georgian theatre existing anywhere in the world today. Performances in the theatre became irregular from 1830 and, in the parlance of the English theatre, it went "dark" for a time.

The building was let as auction rooms in 1848, when wine was stored in the pit area below ground level. It was rediscovered by accident in the late 1950s, after someone decided to examine the lower levels beneath the existing modern floors of what was an old warehouse and was astounded at his findings. In 1960, a trust was formed as a non-profit organisation, which launched a public appeal to raise funds for the restoration of the theatre, following which, the theatre again opened for performances in 1963.

With a Grade I listing already attached to the building and its contents, in 2002, an extensive restoration programme produced an outstanding reconstruction, attached to a completely upgraded, modern building. The theatre retains its unique character of an eighteenth century playhouse, the detail of which transports visitors back in time two and a quarter centuries.

The Culloden Tower (right) was erected to celebrate the victory of George II over the Jacobites in 1745.
Its carved woodwork and plasterwork was restored by The Landmark Trust in 1982.
It was built by John York, a staunch supporter of the Hanoverian Kings and one of Richmond's two Members of Parliament of the time.

6
The Military Connection

The Alma Barracks

The Alma barracks, standing at the top of Gallowgate, was built in the period 1875-77 as a headquarters building for the Green Howards (The Prince of Wales Own), originally the 19th Regiment of Foot. In 1982, the abandoned buildings were used as an approved school, but have since been completely renovated and carefully modernised to provide residential accommodation overlooking the town.

Originally raised in1688, the regiment became known as the 19th (1st North Riding of Yorkshire) Regiment of Foot in 1782. It was re-named in 1744 after its colonel, Sir Charles Howard. In 1902 it was re-designated as Alexandra, Princess of Wales Own (Yorkshire Regiment), recruiting from the north east area, but particularly from North Yorkshire. It was expanded in number for the duration of the First World War and served with distinction in many theatres of war; the Western front, Gallipoli and Italy.

It was increased in size again for the Second World War, when twelve battalions served with distinction. In the 'post war' years, the regiment served in many areas of emergency: Malaya, Afganistan, Suez, Cyprus, Belize, and Northern Ireland; also in the Falklands war, the first Gulf War and Bosnia. Since 1900, the men of The Green Howards have been awarded a total of sixteen Victoria Crosses for gallant action under fire.

Catterick Garrison

Throughout its history, the castle has had a military connotation but has not always been occupied by a military presence. This was not the case at the time of the outbreak of First World War hostilities however, as at that time it housed a group of militia commanded by Lord Robert Baden-Powell who, in 1908, founded the world-wide Scouting movement for boys (with a later spin-off movement for girls headed by his wife).

In 1914, Baden-Powell knew that the country desperately needed a new and specialised training facility for soldiers to improve its chances in modern warfare and suggested the present site of the Catterick Garrison as suitable for the purpose. Having agreed to his suggestion, the government issued an order on 12 August 1914 for work to be undertaken on the construction of the 'camp', initially for a temporary facility, comprising several areas of wooden huts. However, given the exigencies of that dreadful war, its 'temporary' tag was soon abandoned. In fact, most of the original wooden huts, erected at that time were (as the author knows, only too well) still in everyday use as military accommodation 50 years later.

Barrack room lines, about 1948.

Richmond Road, Catterick Camp, 1930s.

The garrison, named Catterick Camp, was completed in October 1915. Being only some two miles from the centre of Richmond, with its perimeter only about a mile away, the camp has always had a close affinity with the town and is often acknowledged as being a satellite community to Richmond. The wooden hut accommodation throughout the camp consisted of double ten bed huts, connected by a shared brick-built ablutions annex, which extended across the front of each hut to contain the non-commissioned officers' accommodation.

Each hut was in the charge of a junior non-commissioned officer, who

Catterick Road, late 1920s before the White shops were built.

slept in a separate room with a small fireplace. The wooden huts were not centrally heated in the modern sense, but had a single coal or wood fired cast iron stove (only lit in the evenings) situated centrally between the bottom eight beds of each hut. Those nearest the stove roasted and those further away froze.

Sandes Soldiers Home, 1940s.

In summer the accommodation was adequate and relatively comfortable, but in the colder periods of the year, especially when the wind from the North Sea blew into the camp's exposed location, the huts were cold, permanently damp, draughty and extremely uncomfortable. After duties, often in the open, soldiers preferred to congregate in communal areas of mess halls, or the NAFFI. They also tended to migrate in large numbers to the relative delights of Richmond, and used the wooden barrack rooms only for sleeping.

Catterick Camp Theatre, 1940s.

Morning and evening washing, shaving and kit cleaning in the shared ablutions annex was often torture, especially in the winter months, on wet, bare concrete floors; with sparse hot water supplied from a centrally, camp-sited boiler room, with little or no insulation on distribution piping. Shower/bath facilities were also centrally sited in each camp area and were only available at limited times each day.

Plate-laying gang for Catterick Camp railway construction. These men were too old or young for enlistment.

Conditions generally at Catterick Camp were so bad in the early 1920s, that one soldier wrote: 'Of all the bleak, windswept camps, the Curragh was bad; Bally Kinlar, Worlds End was worse; but Catterick is even stormier, wilder than them all!'

The G.O.C. General Harrington sent an appeal to the Sandes Charity organisation on behalf of his soldiers at the camp, asking "Would Miss Sandes give me a Soldiers' Home?" The charity had previously excelled in the provision of rest homes for garrisoned soldiers serving in postings abroad, in which they could enjoy periods

This internally much altered building, standing on the corner of Horne Road appears to be the only remnant of the original wooden huts of Catterick Camp remaining today. Externally, with the exception of the central bricked area and the entrance on its left side, it is still as it was in the mid 1950s, when it served as the Guardroom of 7th Training Regt Royal Signals. The cell block was at the far end of the building. Today it serves as an administration building for a transport park.

This building was the Sandes Soldier's Rest Home until it closed in 1983. It contained a variety of much valued and used facilities such as: canteen, library, games room, swimming pool and accommodation for servicemen and their families. Given its closeness to the camp hospital it became an important place of rest for family members visiting their sick/injured service relatives. The building is now used as a training facility.

of peaceful rest and recreation – reading, swimming and various games such as billiards, table tennis and the like. It took time to attract the necessary funds, but subsequently, the charity was allocated a site next to the camp hospital, with a 99-year lease at £150 per year. The Sandes Rest Home opened in 1928. It provided a valuable haven for thousands of soldiers (and nurses from the hospital) in its time, but closed its doors in 1983, afterwards being taken over by the Army and used as an advanced training centre.

Towards the end of the 1914-18 war, the camp area was used to house 5,000 German prisoners of war who were put to work on camp building improvements and general road-building programmes. It was at that time that the road between the garrison and the railway station at Richmond was laid and finished by them.

Given the prevailing conditions at the camp, it was little wonder when; in the months following the Armistice of 11 November 1918, when war-weary men were returning in their thousands from far-flung battlefields; their resistance to infection at its lowest; Spanish influenza swept through the country and especially through Army establishments like the much hated Catterick, causing the deaths of hundreds of soldiers. It may have been co-incidence, but in 1921, it was decided to retain Catterick as a permanent facility and work started to improve the facilities of the camp. In 1923, additional land was acquired and the camp boundaries were enlarged. From that time on, brick-built, centrally heated barrack blocks appeared throughout the enlarging camp and the old huts began to be phased-out. Although their total clearance was to take many more years to complete.

In 1924, it was decided to install the Royal Corps of Signals training facility at Catterick, thereafter the camp became known as the 'Home of the Royal Signals', and was to remain so until the last permanent Royal Signals Squadron left Catterick in 2014. It is still, and will always be regarded as a spiritual home base by all ex-Signals Veterans.

Catterick Camp was fully operational by 1934-5, which was fortuitous, given the outbreak of war again only four years later.

A copy of a 1930s postcard, showing the original Catterick Camp cinema on the Horne Road/Catterick Road crossroads, opposite the 'White Shops'. It was later demolished and replaced by the Ritz Cinema, which was opened on 21 December 1940, and which closed in mid-1977, due to low attendances.

Today the garrison is the largest British Army garrison in the world, having an average population of approximately 13,000 and covering an area of some 2,400 acres. Within current plans for the establishment, its total population is expected to expand to over 25,000 by 2020, and a recent £25 million scheme of re-development for the garrison central area, containing an hotel, cinema, several retail outlets, as well as fast food outlets and bars, will, together with the existing supermarket area of retail facility, make it a very attractive shopping

Marching through the town for the Freedom of Richmond awarded to the Royal Signals, 2014, (photograph courtesy of Robert (Boom) Moore, Royal Signals Association).

As a result of military re-organisation, after 90 years being stationed at Catterick, the last remaining Squadron of Royal Signals personnel left the Catterick Garrison.
To honour the occasion, Richmond invested the Corps with the Freedom of Richmond at a parade at which the Corps Colonel-in-Chief, HRH Princess Anne graciously took the salute.
(photographs courtesy of Robert (Boom) Moore, Royal Signals Association).

venue for many in the surrounding area, including many Dales residents.

Although Catterick Garrison is fast becoming a town in its own right, it will perhaps always be thought of as connected to Richmond. Its links traditionally have always been to the town, where its recreation and other off-duty facilities have been eagerly sought after by the average, off-duty 'squaddie'. Richmond has also actively fostered this relationship, as was recently illustrated by the Freedom of Richmond award to the Royal Signals given at the time of HRH Princess Anne's visit on 11 September 2014.

Above, the relatively new Darlington College, a further education establishment, which was recently built on part of the garrison site. It stands on land which at one time, was part of the railway which served the camp, until the line was closed as a result of the Beeching re-organisation of the railways in the 1960s.

The camp centre roundabout – the railway originally extended through the centre of the roundabout.

From its inception, the camp was served by its own rail connection to the London and North Eastern Railway system. It connected the camp centre with the main line via a branch line to Catterick Bridge Station on the Darlington to Richmond Branch Line. It was mainly used for the passage of goods to the camp, running on down from the area shown, to cross the roundabout at the Garrison Centre. It also ran week-end leave trains, which left the camp from the grassed area shown to the front of the college on Friday afternoons; the returning train left from Kings Cross, London at midnight on Sundays, arriving at the camp at 5:30 a.m. each Monday. The route of the old rail track is now a footway beside the Catterick Road, down past Colburn and Walkerville. From

Colburn it forms part of the Coast to Coast long distance path and crosses the River Swale on the original Garrison Railway bridge at Catterick Bridge.

On 4 February 1944, four unfortunate soldiers were working in a laden munitions rail truck, parked in a siding close to Catterick Bridge Railway Station, when the truck contents suddenly exploded, causing their instant disintegration and enormous damage locally. In all, twelve people were killed, including the station master and 102 others were injured as a result of the blast. Seven houses, the Station Hotel, the adjacent café and the goods yard offices were all destroyed. The blast was heard for several miles' distance from the site.

The multi-million Princes Gate retail shopping area at the garrison's centre.

The author is indebted to the Garrison Sergeant Major, Mr Saul, for his courteous permission to photograph within the garrison area at a time of heightened emergency status.

At the time of writing, the garrison houses the 4th Mechanised 'Black Rats' Brigade.

7
The River Swale

The Nine Standards

The named River Swale begins at a point east of Keld, where Great Sleddale Beck joins Birkdale Beck. Its waters rise from the flanks of Nine Standards Rigg, the main watershed between the eastern and western flowing rivers of northern England.

The Nine Standards cairns are the particular interest of the Friends of Nine Standards, who are developing and working on a project to protect and maintain the feature, while at the same time, establish its true history. The website at www.ninestandards.eu/project.html is of enormous interest and is well worth visiting. The group has raised money to have non-intrusive archaeological work carried out and have carried out extensive research and think that the cairns have been repaired, added to, demolished and re-instated over at least the past nine centuries, since they were claimed as a territorial boundary by Gilbert de Gant (whose ancestor was Walter, William the Conqueror's nephew) in about 1138 as part of his imposition of Forest Law. It must be considered as very doubtful, that he would have ordered the building of nine large cairns as an estate boundary, having instead no doubt taken advantage of an already existing feature as an established and recognisable boundary marker.

Given this possibility, coupled with the existence of much localised Bronze Age evidence, it is entirely possible that the origin of the 'Nine Standers' referred to in the twelfth century Gilbert de Gant document, is at least Bronze-Age. The Friends of Nine Standards hope that in time, they will be able to discover more about this enigmatic landscape feature of the upper dale.

The waters of the River Swale rise high in the Yorkshire Dales, fed from several tributary becks, one of which is Birkdale Beck, seen above beside the road from the head of Swaledale to Kirkby Stephen, at a height of some 420 metres above sea level. Evidence of receding glaciations can be seen quite clearly from this point. The elevated catchment area provides a high proportion of the River Swale's downstream flow.

High in the Pennines above Keld, Ravenseat is situated on a drovers route which was used from medieval times for cattle from the Border counties to be driven south to York and the Midlands. The packhorse bridge is a Grade II listed monument and crosses Whitsundale Beck, which also feeds the River Swale, meeting it in the lower valley, near Keld. The two paintings opposite show Birkdale Beck (top) and Ravenseat (bottom).

The River Swale skirts the town and castle at Richmond below the escarpment and attracts many visitors throughout the year. The falls situated below the castle are spectacular, especially after rainfall higher up the dale from which it comes. The river has powered mills of varying forms and usage for the town and its religious houses through the ages. The river also carried the town's waste products away for many centuries before the modern waste water treatment plant was installed adjacent to the old railway bridge at Easby. The most heavily contaminated outfall from the town to the river occurred opposite the railway station, at the bottom of the existing lane behind St Mary's Parish Church, which extends downhill to the Swale from Frenchgate. It was at this spot that the town's medieval Ducking Stool was located, to be used as punishment for scolding wives and fraudulent vendors of bread, ale and other consumables as well as minor law-breakers, both civil and ecclesiastical.

Not withstanding its spectacular, wild beauty, displayed all year round, the River Swale can suddenly rise, to become a raging maelstrom of the most turbulent water. Its violent power can be determined from the view above of a placid water flow below the Foss at Richmond. The jumble of rocks seen have been torn from the river bed and the face of the waterfall steps by the violence of storm water descending the river, to be then tossed about by the rushing water, despite many of them weighing several tons each. The abject misery caused by such events to Dales people in the late eighteenth and nineteenth centuries is described in some detail later in the book.

The photograph above shows severe bank erosion from high water washing established tree roots clear of their supporting soil. Tree growth on both river banks continues to serve as a buttress against river widening and encroachment.

Richmond's riverside undergoes a spectacular transformation in its autumn colours.

The River Swale is not always tranquil!

SWALEDALE

For two thousand years and more, the fields above the valley floor,
Below the hanging edge and mist hid, moody moor,
Have hid beneath their emerald turf, the signs of early man.
The Age of Bronze leaves little now, save some levelled sward,
Where once stood smoking, circled hutments, girt by outlined furrows,
Hacked-out by hand, for some long forgotten purpose.
Now, the dale contains the names of yore, of Angles and of Norse,
Who strode inland from the sea, with sword in bloody hand,
To leave their mark in garth and thwaite, upon this patterned land.

Look up to misted morning moors, beyond the closed-in fields and farms.
Wait; and watch the while, to see the swirling whiteness lift, its thinning arms
Embracing the warming summer sun, its clinging veil
Clearing from treetop and faintly purpling ling
Watch the shifting shadows shorten, the cloud shadows scurry
From wall to wall, as the sun climbs from its eastern rest,
To reach its zenith above the southern flank.
Lie back, look and listen, as a twittering skylark flutters high
And trickling, chattering water flows-on by.

Sheep, grazing fells and upland places, mournfully call their lambs to heal
When, disturbed by booted walker, or when stormy shadows steal
Across a summer sky and tinkling beck turns to tumbling torrent.
The chattering grouse call, fluttering over ling and old, bronzed bracken,
While overhead, the hungry rook soars beneath a racing cloud.
The wind blows fresh through these upland fields; the rain falls sweet.
In winter, driving snow drifts and lingers long, turning white stone, whiter still
On smoke wreathed, stone walled, stone roofed cottage
And newer Dalesman tends his stock with older fortitude and courage.

Where placid cart-horse, plodding, pulled the plough to turn its rich, brown furrow
In stone walled, stone strewed fields, now tractors cut and harrow
Amid seemingly square and solid, grey-stone barns.
Grey stores and shelters, scattered within winding, watered pastures,
Distantly appearing as giant's gaming-pieces on a living board of verdant green.
Dalesman and darting dog comb brackened fells with whistles shrill,
Driving home reluctant sheep, with lambs for market, or for marking,
From long walled, deep gullied fellside, or moss strewn moor,
And from where streams of singing water cascade to the valley floor.

Swollen by the sudden storm and winter's driving rain,
Down and down, through gill and beck, these surging waters drain,
Tumbling over whinstone shelf, to pool awhile in darkened hollow.
Free again; and on, they chuckle past the scattered scree,
Beneath the wind-blown, stunted tree, to run on, past the well trod path
Left by years and countless sheep and boots of trudging walkers.
On past farmstead, under stone arched bridge and gulley,
These rich, bronzed waters, tinged with peat 'neath soggy moss and heather,
Meet as the meandering Swale to tumble on together.

From Birkdale, Stonesdale, Lovely Seat; from Gunnerside and Satron Moor;
From Crackpot and the Arkle Dale, the peaty waters pour
Following their ancient course through gorge and busy narrows,
Past white stone crags and wall bound pastures green,
The waters wend their winding, stone strewn way, 'neath high arched bridge
From where, amid the glinting ripples and secret dark brown depths,
A sudden silver-sided flash reveals a turning trout.
On, through deep and shaded wood, the waters leave their dale
By Richmond's rising ramparts, to enter York's broad vale.

In times past, countless teams of lead-laden, cropping, clopping horses
Driven by drover's whip and word from Swaledale's watercourses,
Onward, through grey stoned village, towards the sea, where wooden ships
Waited on the tide, to take the heavy harvest across the waves by wind-filled sail.
Fells carry still, the limestone scars upstream from Richmond's keep,
Where peaty waters thrash their way from rock strewn gill and beck;
Fells, which once rang loud with miners' melodious pick and hammer.
Men, toughened as the stone on which they worked, wresting meagre living,
Fearing no man; only God, whom they thanked each day for giving.

Echoes, softening now, remain in tumbled building; serried, shattered stone;
Washing floor and rusted rail; pit and level overgrown,
But retaining still, the lengthening shadow of long departed labour.
Each part, a stark, mute monument to some toiling Dalesman's past;
A history glimpsed, clear, yet fleetingly, in some fading, broken photograph,
Seen cracked and curling, together with his tools, in some museum.
Proud, bewhiskered, work stained men, young and old and older still.
Each one, mutely reflecting their time, but not their motivation,
Their daily toil and occupation, but not their inclination.

Peter Moppet

Swaledale is the most northerly dale of North Yorkshire's Dales and without doubt is the most unspoilt, prettiest dale of them all. It extends east to west, from Nine Standards Rigg on the Cumbria/North Yorkshire border to the administrative centre at the town of Richmond. Its valley road, running mainly along its bottom levels, connects its village communities, the majority of which are sited on the lower, sunny side of the road along the dale. Each community has its own riverside, green meadows and upper dale side summer pastures, (each with its own typical stone-built field barn), bound by ancient drystone walls. Its history is extensive.

Following the death of Alan Rufus, who fathered no legitimate children, the Lordship of Richmond passed in turn to his brothers. In 1098, Stephen of Penthievre, the younger brother, became the 3rd Lord of Richmond. His daughter Maud married Walter of Ghent and took with her, as a dowry, the whole of Swaledale.

The nearest existing village along the dale from Richmond is Grinton and it seems that this particular community took on an importance from that date, as the modern Parish of Grinton officially extends over the whole of upper Swaledale, to include the communities of Grinton; Melbecks (including Feetham, Gunnerside, Kearton, Lodge Green, Low Row, and Pot Ing); Muker (including Angram, Keld, Thwaite, Birkdale, East and West Stonesdale, Oxhop, Ravenseat and Satron); and Reeth (including Fremington and Healaugh). Certainly, until a church was built at Muker, the Grinton Church, was the official burial point for the whole dale area and corpses of dead residents of the dale were regularly carried from all along its considerable length, on what is now commonly known as the Corpse Road for burial in Grinton Churchyard.

In the early eighteenth century, Swaledale was described as, '...the largest tract of waste in South Britain... There are only four acres of arable land and 60 acres of woods and plantations, while 12,919 acres are permanent grass, the remainder being moorland...' Obviously much has changed since then. Modern farming practices and equipment have improved the land and its output, although it still favours animal husbandry, mainly with sheep, rather than the widespread arable type farming of the farms beyond Richmond in the Vale of Mowbray.

The dale has its own breed of hardy Swaledale sheep, with prominent horns and mainly black faces which can be seen everywhere throughout the dale at all times of the year and the face of the Swaledale has been adopted as the official logo for the Yorkshire Dales National Park. Without any doubt at all, the long practice the hill farmers of running sheep in the dales and the ovine habit of cropping grass close to the surface, has transformed the dales into the areas of beauty that we see today.

8
Historic Occupation of Swaledale

Evidence of the early occupation of Swaledale, before the Bronze Age, has been found in some small, but quite specific evidence. The earliest humans were nomadic hunters and gatherers so they did not plan for long-term occupation and, in any case the inhospitable climate and geography of the dale would have made it an uncomfortable place to live. Recent opinion based upon archaeological finds, points to the dale having been occupied by Mesolithic people; giving a date for the earliest known human occupation, or incursion into the dale of around 2,700 BC, followed by Neolithic and early Bronze Age people settling from the period around 1,800 BC.

Beneath the heather of the fells and moorland tops, parallel (coaxial) field boundaries have been discovered, and no doubt many more are still to be found. These boundaries are thought to be of Bronze Age construction and have been linked to the typical practices of the Bronze Age period of field stone clearance and the construction of related stone cairn fields. Many indications have also been found of Bronze Age round house sites and other signs of contemporary occupation on the higher ground of the dale. The extent of the recent finds has drawn a conclusion that the Bronze Age occupation was fairly extensive and at least covered the lower, eastern end of the dale, around Grinton, Marrick and Harkerside. The study continues as more evidence is uncovered.

Of the Iron Age and Romano-British periods of occupation, much has been discovered and gives an impression of a settled, productive farming community, which existed and thrived in Swaledale for over half a millennium. There are sites of interest visible today which give distinct impressions of Iron Age living in the dale. Grinton prehistoric mounds are two mounds of glacial moraine, left behind by a retreating glacier, on which were sited round houses from the Iron Age. Evidence was found at Healaugh of a small house cluster from the period and below Whitecliffe Scar, a larger settlement appears to have existed. How Hill at Downholme and Maiden Castle at Harkerside near Grinton are outstanding examples of Iron Age occupation, although the exact character and use of Maiden Castle in the period with its stone approach avenue is unclear.

Round houses of both historic periods were commonly built on level platforms found naturally on the dale sides, or excavated by hand for the purpose. As one travels through the dale, many such platforms can be seen, empty now, but perhaps at one time they held a small community, or extended family of ancient farmers. It is also not beyond the realms of possibility that many similar locations in Swaledale, now accommodating the homes and outbuildings of modern farms, were once home to an ancient family.

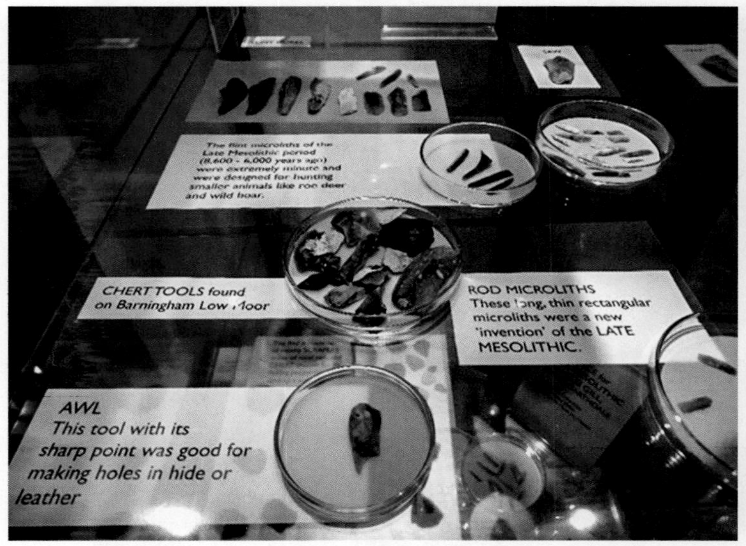

Mesolithic finds from Swaledale in the ??? Museum, Richmond?

Above the remains of Maiden Castle, which was an Iron-Age fortified enclosure on Harkerside, as seen from the B6270 road at Healaugh.
Below, Maiden Castle, western ditch and rampart.

Above, Maiden Castle, western ditch and rampart, below, remains of the stone-lined approach avenue.

Above, Howe Hill, Downholme. Below, Iron Age enclosure under Whitecliffe Scar, above East Applegarth. Photographs courtesy of the Swaledale Museum, Reeth.

Above, Iron Age enclosure under Whitecliffe Scar, above East Applegarth.
Below, the Grinton Mounds – the archaeology of the western mound has been compromised by the installation of a Cold War observation antenna.

The settlements of Grinton, Fremington, Reeth and Stainton, are all Anglo-Saxon in origin. The initial incursion of the Angles from northern Europe into Britain occurred in the mid-fifth century, when they arrived by long boat and made their way up the eastern rivers and began to settle and farm along the river banks. Swaledale was occupied by them, along the lower reaches of the Swale, later in about the early eighth century. The Angles preferred to live in organised settlements with houses grouped together as a village, bringing safety in numbers and an enclosed central area where livestock could be brought in times of threat. Reeth is a clear example of this principle and another surviving example can be seen at Scorton, five miles to the east of Richmond, beside the Swale as it enters the Vale of Mowbray.

Vikings from Norway and Denmark periodically raided the shores of Britain in search of slaves and silver to plunder for many decades from about 789 AD, when the first of the raiders was reported in the *Anglo-Saxon Chronicles*. Eager for good farming land, which could not be found by many Viking sons in their home countries, they settled in Ireland first, before crossing the Irish Sea to enter the dales of Britain from the west in about 950 AD. The upper part of Swaledale was settled by them and resulted in the Norse based names of the dale's current western communities, such as Thwaite, Keld, Ravenseat and Stonesdale. They preferred to live apart, clearing living space in locations among the upland scrub and woodland and, as was their custom, migrating upwards to the fells above with their livestock in the summer months. The present character of upper Swaledale with scattered, fairly isolated communities, stems from this predilection on the part of the early Norse settlers.

Accessible remains of the Romano-British period are very few in Swaledale. The existing remains of the Roman Fort and Vicus at Catterick Bridge were almost fully excavated in 1959/60, but were re-interred in order to preserve them. The structure illustrated above is part of an easily-missed, quite long length of well buttressed bund wall, (in imminent danger of being overwhelmed and irreparably damaged by the tree and undergrowth of the river-side). It was built by the Roman soldiers of Catteractonium, to protect the Vicus, (the small civilian settlement outside the walls of the soldier's garrison), from flooding by the adjacent River Swale. The modern Coast to Coast long distance footpath extends alongside it, only a few feet away from unsuspecting walkers.

The remains of Ellerton Abbey.

The Norman Conquest of England in 1066, caused great rebellion in Yorkshire in particular and King William's response was one of great severity and brutality. Simeon of Durham; an English chronicler and monk of Durham Priory, wrote an account of the 'Harrowing of the North' in about 1100, saying: 'So great a famine prevailed that men, compelled by hunger devoured human flesh, that of horses, dogs and cats... It was horrific to behold human corpses decaying in the houses, the streets and the roads; for no one was left to bury them in the ground, all being cut-off by the sword or by famine.'

Houses, crops, all food and grain seed, cattle, sheep, horses and any other animals were burnt. Throughout the northern region, thousands of people were slaughtered outright, or died a slow death through famine. The lucky ones ran away to safety elsewhere, but northern England was devastated and took years to recover. Swaledale became something of a wilderness for several decades afterwards.

After Walter of Ghent received the area as his wife's dowry, circumstances in the dale began to improve. The first monastic buildings began to emerge on land given as grants; and large areas of Swaledale became a hunting reserve for the enjoyment of the Norman overlords.

Despite Scottish raiders who rampaged through the dale several times, the impoverished dale began to prosper again and prosperity continued until 1349, when the Black Death plague swept through the dale, killing two thirds of the population. The lead mining industry of Swaledale, always active to varying extent from Roman times, began to develop again in the aftermath of the plague and gradually brought about the resumption of a thriving dale-wide community.

Marrick Priory was established between 1140 and 1160 as a Benedictine Nunnery. Following the General Dissolution of Henry VIII, the site became a farm. Its church was used for worship by the local population, until it fell into disuse in 1948. In 1970, the church building was occupied as an Outdoor Educational and Residential Centre for young persons, giving them experience in team building and all outdoor pursuits.

9
Lead Mining

Notwithstanding the outward beauty of the Yorkshire Dales, it has its dark side hidden away in side valleys, gills and watercourses. Lead mining in Swaledale has taken place for many centuries past. We know from the evidence of ingots of lead bearing Roman inscriptions of Emperors Hadrian and Trajan found in North Yorkshire (one of them at Hurst in Swaledale), that mining in Roman times took place. Evidence also surfaces to indicate that mining was being performed when the Ghent family lands passed to Crown ownership during the reign of Henry II, for in 1219, a mandate was issued, securing the King's workmen in Swaledale (miners), the right to continue to work unmolested, as they had done under the king's rule. In 1599, a lead mine at Grinton was specifically mentioned in legal documentation in connection to the Crown and lead mines at Grinton, Whitesides, Harkerside and Fremington were legally leased in 1628.

Lead is a naturally occurring heavy-metal found in ore form known as galena, which is an amalgam of lead, silver and zinc in varying quantities. As with all minerals, it was formed by geological and volcanic action working deep underground, forcing mineral salt-laden water through cracks, fissures and faults in the upper rock strata, where the salts leached out to solidify within the voids as mineral deposits.

Throughout history, lead has been sought after as a result of its malleability, comparatively low melting point and durability. It has been used through the ages for sealing joints in masonry, bonding iron to masonry, waterproofing roofing, and for water piping, where its character in sheet form lends itself to easy bending and forming without fear of cracking, making it the ideal material for proofing water carrying vessels. The Romans valued it, mediaeval architects valued it and its use in building projects continues to the present day.

Lead deposits in and around Swaledale were extensive and relatively easy to access from the surface. Over time and after the surface deposits disappeared, the ore became both difficult to find and hard to mine. Lead from Yorkshire and especially from Swaledale has been used in all the major castle and church building programmes in Britain and has also been regularly exported to Europe since the Middle Ages. Trains of lead laden pack-horses have been led out of the dale, through Richmond for hundreds of years on their way to waiting water transport at Yarm and Boroughbridge. In the history of warfare, lead has played a major role in the manufacture of ammunition since the advent of guns and gunpowder.

Mining operations in any form for any mineral or underground deposit have always been fraught with dangers. Ore deposits are not easily found and ore extraction in any confined space has never been easy and has always been hazardous. When deposits are found, they are often massively convoluted in their disposition in the rock strata and can be extremely sparse or huge in thickness. Their levels can be, and often are, coincidental with water levels, making mining dirty, unhealthy, and uncomfortable as well as dangerous.

During the Middle Ages, when land was being granted by the Crown and by local overlords to religious communities such as Fountains Abbey, Reivaulx and York, much, if not all mineral mining operations, especially for lead throughout the dales area, were controlled, organised and directed by these great houses. They owned the land, issued rights and leases to mine and collected large shares of profits as royalties. The devastating effects of the great plagues on the country's population, as well as Henry VIII's General Dissolution Act (when roof lead from destroyed monastic buildings flooded the market), caused the first fluctuations in the demand for lead in the early and late Middle Ages. Low demand continued until the time of migration of much of the remaining population to towns and cities in search of work following the Agrarian Revolution and the Enclosure Acts. That and the gradual increase in industrial activity up to and into the age of the industrial revolution, brought about a steady increase in demand for the metal.

As time progressed, the ore required deeper operations to extract, which caused greater difficulties in handling both ore and waste rock spoil. Deeper mining also meant more water problems, requiring pumping, or adits (sideways bored tunnels opened into the fellside from the internal water level) to drain the water away by gravity. If a natural fault point was reached where the ore vein disappeared suddenly, hundreds of tons of rock

Fells landscaped by 'hushing' at Gunnerside Gill, Swaledale.

spoil could have to be moved in a search for the vein's continuance. Sometimes fruitless, such a catastrophe could result in the mine's closure. In such cases, other accessible veins had to be discovered quickly and one of the ways in which this was done was by 'hushing'. A large dam would be constructed above a likely surface location, behind which, thousands of tons of water would be allowed to accumulate. When the amount of water was judged to be sufficient, the dam would be destroyed, allowing the water to descend with tremendous force, washing away any rock and vegetation, creating a huge artificial valley in which, hopefully a new ore vein would be found.

The introduction of gunpowder for mining operations in the seventeenth century made the extraction of rock spoil and the valuable ore easier, but it brought with it obvious additional hazards for the miner. It lowered extraction costs to such an extent that people with cash to invest, rushed to place their funds in the hands of the mine operating companies. With the additional capital, mines expanded and as machinery such as engine driven pumps and ventilation were invented and became available to purchase, mine owners were quickly attracted to the ideas of mechanised mining and the lowered costs which were promised by the improved and quicker extraction circumstances.

Mining families worked incredibly hard. Conditions at the mine face and on the ore processing and washing areas were worse than arduous and a day's work involved extremely hard labour for long hours in terrible conditions and in all weathers. In order to commence this hard labour, many workers were expected to toil for miles uphill from their homes to their place of work; then having expended so much energy for a full day's shift, tired and soaked to the skin; they would have to toil again downhill to sleep.

Boys started work at ten years of age, usually employed on the washing and sorting floors, where ore was washed and crushed by hand to remove rock and crystal impurities. As middle to late teenagers, they would be taken into the mine to work as part of a mining gang, where they worked clearing rock spoil, erecting staging and stacking waste rock – all by hand.

Wages were less than £1 per week for a miner at the end of the 1800s; boys underground were paid less.

Grinton lead smelting mill

The boys with surface jobs were paid even less, with the youngest receiving less than a shilling (5 pence) per day. Women also worked on the ore processing areas and were paid less than the boys.

Family income was at best irregular and always low and unreliable. If work was available, they earned, if not, they were sent home. Miners were forced to provide additional support to feed their families from small-holdings which they would work on after their day at the mine, often until well into the hours of darkness. If they could maintain a meagre vegetable supply in this way, with perhaps a pig and a milk producing cow, they were well-off; but many could not and had to rely on poaching or local hill farmers for additional employment for cash. The home produced knitting opportunities from men like Caleb Readshaw from Richmond, for hats, gloves, stockings and scarves, enabled a complete family (young and old) to contribute towards extra income, and stories are told today that families, including the men, could be seen knitting while trudging up footpaths to the mines.

Lead Smelting

Of all the trades connected to lead mining, that of smelting the ore in the production of ingot lead was perhaps the worst.

Given the difficulties of the terrain in which the mining took place and the costs involved in transporting great loads of heavy, extracted ore any distance, each different mining location throughout the dales had its own dedicated smelter either adjacent to it, or in reasonably close proximity to the mine. Each smelting mill was equipped with ore storage; coal, coke and peat storage (and in some cases a coking kiln); a water supply and waterwheel arrangement for working air bellows; not less than two furnace hearths and a chimney, or flu, by which furnace heat and fumes could be naturally vented away from the mill.

The practice of smelting, consisted of several separate activities. Firstly, the ore had to be separated from as much impurity as could be managed by pulverising it by hand with heavy hammers to the size of garden peas and then washing the product by agitation in water. This made the heavy ore sink to the bottom of washing

Above and top of next page, Grinton Mill's exhaust flu, venting most of its smoke and dangerous fumes, extended uphill to rise some 60 metres, terminating at a chimney on Cogden Moor.

baskets, allowing the rock and other impurities like fluorspar, calcite and other crystal attachments to rise to the surface, to be discarded on the waste tips. The ore then had to be drained before being taken to the furnace. The smelting hearth on which the ore was heated to melt the lead content was a large pillow shaped iron casting, which was dished and shaped with a drain to one side, enabling the impurities to be scraped away, and allowing the molten lead to be ladled into ingot moulds.

The smelting mill at Grinton, which has been renovated and is currently used as an animal shelter, is the most complete smelter left standing today in the Yorkshire Dales. Although its interior is incomplete, it shows exactly what conditions inside a typical smelting mill were like. Floor areas and furnace hearths were entirely open to atmosphere and heat, smoke and fumes from the process had to rise some fifteen to twenty feet, before being induced into the extraction flu by a natural draught created by open doors and a chimney system which rose uphill for a considerable distance.

The wheel room at Grinton Mill – a top-fed waterwheel sited here operated the bellows.

Commonly, chimney flues rose uphill for half a mile or more. They were equipped with a condensing chamber about half way along their length, which would have been filled with bracken and tree branches on which oxidised lead particles deposited by the fumes were deposited. Periodically, during smelter maintenance periods, boys with little or no protection were sent into the flu and the condenser to scrape and brush-off and collect the accumulated concretion of red and white lead. Afterwards it would be washed, dried and pulverised, for sale and use in the paint and cosmetics industry.

The author is well experienced with lead/zinc smelting processes and has designed the electrical power, distribution and controls for smelting plants for this purpose throughout the world. In the modern industry, plants and equipment are designed to extract, cleanse and contain dangerous fumes. All workers and visitors are supplied with and are expected to wear special masks in all locations within a works, preventing the inhalation of toxic lead fumes from the process. Our forebears in the industry were not as fortunate and were not considered beyond being a working facility.

The details of the 1851 census for Swaledale demonstrate quite clearly that the lead mining and smelting operations of the dales were an extreme hazard to those who worked in them. In 1851, lead output from the dales was at its greatest and the 1851 census return shows statistics of an industry in full employment.

Above, one of the two open hearth furnace locations at Grinton Mill. The lighter colouring of its lower area is the result of its having been partially buried for years, since it stopped working.

Left and below, ore hearth and lead ingot (pig) mould from the Grinton Smelt Mill (photographs courtesy Richmond Museum).

Sadly, though, from the statistics shown in the census of 1864, the Kinaird Commission reported that males of Swaledale who worked in the mining industry were likely to die significantly younger than men employed in other occupations. The figures demonstrated that the average age of death for lead miners and smelters at the time was 46.67 years; whereas, the average death age of those in other occupations in the same area was 60.79 years.

Lead poisoning has been known and guarded against as a work and environmental hazard since the time of the ancient Greeks, but the minute quantities necessary to create havoc with the human body were not fully quantified until well into the twentieth century. With so many scattered smelting

The remains of the Old Gang smelting mill beside Hard Level Gill, between Arkengarthdale and Swaledale

Lead mine ore tub for the horse level (from the Lawrence Barker collection, Swaledale Museum). Note the narrow width to negotiate the equally narrow tunnels excavated when following ore seams.

plants working throughout the dale, each one freely liberating lead fumes into the atmosphere, Swaledale, at the height of production would have been a very dangerous area to live in. Lead affects the successful working of the body of all vertebrates and is toxic to the heart, bones, intestines, kidneys and liver, as well as the nervous and reproductive systems. Routes of infection include contaminated air, water, soil and food. Therefore, as well as those mining and smelting the metal, everyone living within range of the dale's lead industry would have run the risk of contamination to varying levels.

The Old Gang Mill remains are perhaps the most starkly picturesque of any left in the dales. Looking carefully at the remaining structures, one can visualise the whole process of eighteenth and nineteenth century smelting, from ore storage, through sorting, cleaning, grading; then from melting to pig production. The mill's chimney flu rises approximately

180 metres from the mill furnace area, across Healaugh Side, terminating at its chimney site above Healaugh Crag.

Above, Old Gang flu arch.

Left, example of a lead pig and ingot mould (photograph courtesy of Reeth Museum).

Typical miner's tools, boots and hanging candle holders from Lawrence Barker and John Hardy.

Above, a heavy metal 'Bucker', used by women and young boys to pound and crush raw galena ore straight from the mine, prior to its being washed and smelted.

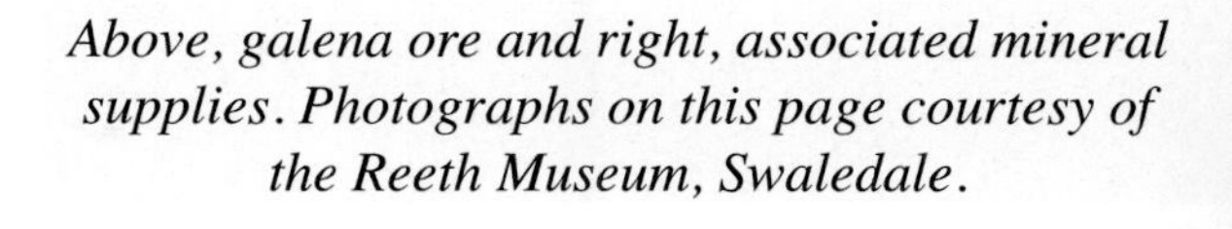

Above, galena ore and right, associated mineral supplies. Photographs on this page courtesy of the Reeth Museum, Swaledale.

10
Farming

Farming has taken place in Swaledale since the early Bronze Age. At that time fields began to be systematically set out and cultivated throughout the dale; work which consumed decades of labour by many families living locally to each area. This entailed the ultra-laborious task of felling trees, clearing the land of stones and rock, clearing scrub and then delineating fields with the cleared stones, which eventually became the now-familiar walls.

Although, as archaeology has established, some arable areas were obviously worked during that time (as they still are today), the majority of land throughout the dale, especially the higher land was, and is despite modern agricultural machinery and methods, favourable in the main, to grass and animal husbandry.

Swaledale ewes.

Sheep, goats, pigs, horses and cattle are bred and graze in the lower pastures, or shelter in the dale's field barns from the onset of winter to the start of the warmer days of spring and summer. Then, the cattle and sheep are herded into the upland pastures, allowing the lower, river fed and watered pastures to grow and ripen the much needed hay crop with which to feed the stock in the winter months.

Initially Bronze Age and Iron Age families produced only what they or their scattered communities needed to live on. As the population of the dale increased over the succeeding centuries and methods of farming improved, some surplus production became available to sell or trade-on to others. Movement of produce required means of transport throughout the dale in both directions. In this way, trackways became roads, river fords

Scar House Farm, Thwaite, a typical uplands farm scene and, below, beef cattle resting and grazing above Keld.

were eventually bridged, and markets were introduced. Businesses grew in several ways as a direct result: carters and carriers; butchers; sool spinners, weavers, millers, carpenters and many other artisan trades, with Reeth as the main centre for most of them.

People needed clothes all year round and wool kept folk warm in the meanest of weather. The dale's wool trade grew enormously very early in its history and occupied its inhabitants as a trade long before the advent

of the lead mining activities. During the seventeenth century, a law was introduced, which required all deceased persons to be buried in woollen shrouds. This created even further demand for the product and a growth in the number of sheep grazing the fields and fells.

From as early as Elizabeth I's time until the demise of the mining interests in the nineteenth century, farming and lead mining occupations were followed side-by-side in the majority of families in the dale. In 1881, it is recorded from the research of John and Marion Hearfield, that a total of 1071 households lived and worked in Swaledale and Arkengarthdale. Assuming that, at that time, an average household would have consisted of approximately seven persons (young and old), the total population of the two related dale's area would have been around 7,500. The stability of numbers at that time indicates a highly productive area, with a population in reasonably full employment, able to support itself from both aspects of occupation – this was not to last.

By 1891, over half of families living in Swaledale had departed from the dale and were not being replaced, as the area had been systematically devastated by repeated catastrophic weather conditions in several of the intervening years and could no longer support them.

The cloudburst over Great Shunnor Fell in 1899 is described in some detail in the section following about the village of Thwaite. Serious winter snowstorms and severe sub-zero temperatures, as well as extraordinarily sudden spring thaws and many severe rainstorms, ravaged Swaledale and Arkengarthdale again and again during the 1890s.

For instance, in 1882: December extra heavy snowfall and severely low temperatures caused the death of hundreds of sheep and two horses; creating massive snowdrifts along the length of the upper dale. For several weeks, movement along and out of the dale was extremely difficult, which made the recovery and feeding of livestock impossibly difficult.

In 1883: January brought unusually high temperatures, which created ultra-rapid thaw conditions, leading to prolonged, serious flooding throughout the dale. Gunnerside, Thwaite, Ivelet bridges and Eskeleth bridge

Rock debris littering the river bed, where Gunnerside Gill enters the River Swale. One can visualise the immense damage caused by such waterborne debris, smashing its destructive way through villages, homes and farms.

in Arkengarthdale were broken and swept away by the tide and ferocity of the downward rush of meltwater. All along the dale, cottages adjacent to the River Swale and its tributary becks were invaded by the floodwater.

It is reported that hundreds of tons of rock-slide completely cut off the Downholme road towards Richmond. Flooding continued, and by February, farmland adjacent to the Swale, all along the dale, had been devastated by encroaching, accumulating debris brought down from the mine workings above the dale by the torrents of meltwater, reportedly turning much productive farmland into virtual wilderness. It was considered that the lead contamination of the soil would cause extensive risk of death to livestock and cost a fortune to successfully clean-up. By March, with bad weather continuing and with very little having been possible to achieve in terms of clean-up; families were severely distressed, with many reduced to extreme poverty.

Swale Bridge, Gunnerside.

In 1884 January again brought about abnormally heavy rainfall throughout North Yorkshire, making all roads impassable. These floods, added again to previous injury on the part of the Swaledale inhabitants, made their lives miserable in the extreme; and from which, it took months for them to recover to anywhere near normal.

In 1886 the January snowfalls were abnormally heavy again, which made extraction and recovery of sheep flocks from accumulated drifts on the fells arduous and dangerous.

March arrived, bringing with it the most severe winter storm conditions ever encountered. For periods of several days on end, farmers and shepherds were unable to work outdoors and flocks and livestock generally had to be left unattended and unfed, with consequent distress and heavy losses. With no let-up in the weather conditions, the dales folk became desperate for some respite, fearful that the spring and early summer crops of badly needed hay would not be forthcoming and also fearful that they would inevitably be forced to buy in fodder for their stock. Families could not obtain fuel supplies for heating and cooking. Consequently, they were

Above ewe and lambs sheltering beside an ancient stone wall.

Left, sheep herding and penning the modern way.

reduced to burning any combustible item available, including doors and furniture. Roads were blocked for weeks, with snow drifts in excess of 30 feet deep. No post could be delivered or sent and no provisions obtained.

By April and May, when the ewes traditionally gave birth to the much needed, valuable lamb production, weather conditions had only marginally improved. New born lambs died in their hundreds and bereft ewes struggled forlornly in the drift-strewn fields.

In 1887 January's remaining heavy snow accumulation was subjected again to extremely rapid thaw conditions, causing the River Swale to rise abnormally and cause flooding in several places. In contrast, by July the lack of rain created extreme drought conditions which took effect over all of the north east of the country. Rivers and tributary becks dried up, with the Swale and Ure rivers reduced to a veritable trickle. Crop production everywhere became impossible to sustain in the quantity required to outlast the approaching winter and stock found difficulty in foraging for food.

Upper Swaledale farming landscape, showing upper and lower pastures, field barns and dry stone dividing walls.

The following year February again brought extreme snowfall, with high winds creating huge snowdrifts. It was impossible to travel any distance and farmers generally found themselves again confined to their homes, with little possibility of going out to feed their livestock. The wintry conditions continued into May which again affected lamb production.

July 1888 saw extensive rain storms, which once more brought tons of water and mine debris cascading down the several watercourses of Swaledale and Arkengarthdale to choke roads, smash through bridges, houses and gardens, smother fields and wash away valuable crops. A great number of bovine and ovine stock was lost on many farms, causing great financial loss to the owners. Once again, farmers despaired of ever recovering their fields and livelihoods.

On the 25 August there was 95mm of rainfall, swelling the rivers and becks, and once again washing away the bridge (and the road) at Gunnerside. Fields were again inundated along the dale, making farmer's lives and livelihoods again tenuous. To cap this sad litany of misery, in 1889, along came the veritable grandfather of all rainstorms which smashed its destructive way through Swaledale and Wensleydale.

Each weather event throughout the 1880s, progressively proved to be the final straw for residents of the dale, creating an exodus towards safer havens and means of employment available in the towns and cities of the more southern counties, or abroad. Many farms were left without tenants and the mining operations throughout the two related dales of Swaledale and Arkengarthdale, already stricken by lower priced imports, suffered, both through severe damage and a lack of available labour. New people were not attracted to move into the dales because the area was considered to be a hazard and not at all profitable.

Goats illustration in coloured pencil

11
Swaledale: The Villages

Keld

Keld is the first village one arrives at when entering Swaledale from the direction of Kirkby Stephen, although the term 'village' rather belies its modern size, as it now consists of a few dwellings and a farm set around a central area. It does have two chapels, (Congregational and Methodist), a school and a Literary Institute. It also has a small hotel/restaurant uphill from the centre, which at one time was a youth hostel. The present community of Keld is small, but in the nineteenth century, when the lead mining industry of the area was in full production, its population was around 6,000.

The name Keld, derives from the Norse word *kelda*, meaning spring or rising water. An apt name, considering that Keld is situated directly above a gorge through which the adjacent River Swale rushes eastwards. There are no less than four major waterfalls within a short walking distance from the village centre, Wan Wath Force; Catrake Force (upper, middle and lower); East Gill Force and the massive Kisdon Force, each of which attracts crowds of visitors annually.

Keld from the footpath to Swinner Gill.

Catrake Upper Falls.

Keld lies at the junction of two major long distance footpaths; the Pennine Way, running south to north, and the Coast to Coast path, normally walked from west to east. The village is also the start of the Corpse Road, which rises over the adjacent Kisdon Hill, dropping down to Thwaite and Muker, before wending its way on towards Grinton at the eastern end of the dale. The village has accordingly become a welcome stopping-off point for hundreds of walkers.

The forlorn remains of Crackpot Hall, the ruined farmhouse high on the dale side, (overlooking Kisdon, the Swale Valley and a distant Muker); and the lead mining remains of Swinner Gill, can be fairly easily reached after a short walk from the village centre, passing East Gill Force on the way. The road to the high altitude Tan Hill Inn rises through West Stonesdale not far from the village, as does also the road to Ravenseat, a remote moorland farm and the site of an ancient pack-horse bridge.

Above, Catrake Force and below East Gill Force, lower cascade.

Above, East Gill Force and below, Kisdon Force, Keld.

Farm Cottage, Keldside, Swaledale.

Aygill Farm, Keld.

Thwaite

The village of Thwaite is situated below Kisdon Hill on the north bank of Thwaite Beck, about three kilometres east of Keld. The name 'Thwaite' is Norse in origin and translated, means an open, level space or clearing. The name indicates that the ancient land, when found and settled by the Norse invaders, arriving from the west into Swaledale in the early tenth century, was still woodland.

Situated on knolls of glacial moraine, immediately to the east of Thwaite centre, the site of an early Iron–Age settlement has been found. The settlement existed within an enclosure formed from an earthen bank and ditch, probably surrounded by a wooden palisade and consisted of a few round-houses of the period. It seems apparent therefore, that before the arrival of the Norse, the immediate area around Thwaite had been cleared and farmed by its Iron-Age inhabitants.

Over the centuries farming has undoubtedly provided the foundation of life for the inhabitants of Thwaite, but as with all of the village communities in Swaledale, the lead mines locally would have provided additional means of employment to many of its people and mining occupations co-existed with those of livestock rearing and minimal arable farming in Thwaite. The village population rose steadily throughout its history, but declined drastically towards the end of the nineteenth Century, due in part to the demise of the mining interests in the dale but also following a series of natural disasters.

The River Swale has always been subject to sudden rise in water levels after rainfall in the dale, and a series of serious flood events in the nineteenth century brought loss and extreme hardship to many of its inhabitants. The floods of 1883, 1888 and 1899, were particularly disastrous and created havoc in Wensleydale and

Above and below, the Buttertubs.

Swaledale. The 1899 event, caused by cloudbursts in the Great Shunner Fell area was particularly serious for Thwaite. It was reported that, on 12 July, the sky blackened over Shunner and hailstones more than an inch in diameter fell, smashing roofs and windows, while rain fell in torrents, rushing down the many watercourses from the fell to engulf the villages in both dales below.

Flood water tore its way through Thwaite, carrying with it boulders individually weighing tons and enormous quantities of rock, soil, sand and pebbles, completely destroying gardens and out-houses; overwhelming fields and livestock and seriously damaging many of the village houses and infrastructure. The village never completely recovered from the event and thereafter, its population gradually dwindled to today's levels, with many of its dwellings becoming holiday cottages.

Thwaite.

On a brighter note, the village was home to the brothers, Richard and Cherry Kearton, who were born in Thwaite in 1862 and 1871 respectively. They became renowned as early pioneers of wildlife photography and produced many books and articles on the subject. Their name is commemorated in that of the Kearton hotel/restaurant, situated in the village centre, from which, one can enjoy a superb view of Kisdon. The village annually hosts visiting walkers and motorists and is an attractive centre for those wishing to enjoy the scenery of the upper dale.

The road to Wensleydale rises just to the east of the village and ascends via Buttertubs Pass and Great Shunner Fell, to drop down to Hawes to the south. The Buttertubs are a series of limestone potholes, created by millennia of water erosion of the surrounding rock, to form spectacularly fluted potholes falling to a depth of around 65 feet. Tradition has it that the name arises from a use of the cool depths of the holes by resting farmers, on their way to Hawes market with their dairy products for sale. The fenced holes are easily accessible from the road, where one or two parking areas have been provided. Buttertubs Pass has been described as the most spectacular road in the country.

Above Thwaite Beck and below, typical Swaledale field barn, Thwaite, with Kisdon in the background.

Above, Bridge Cottage and below, Cliffe Bec falls, Thwaite.

Above, prehistoric settlement site at Thwaite and below, Muker.

Muker

Muker is situated just over one mile away, to the east of Thwaite and stands on the northern bank of Straw Beck, which connects with the River Swale, a few yards downstream from the village centre.

The Church of St Mary the Virgin is central to the village and was established as a parish church, with a consecrated graveyard in 1580, during the reign of Queen Elizabeth I. The newly formed parish, embracing all of the western dale communities of Keld, Thwaite, Angram, Birkdale and West Stonesdale, enabled the inhabitants of these areas to bury their dead relatively locally, dispensing with the arduous task of carrying them across the Corpse Road to Grinton for burial.

Muker, former village school and vicarage.

The new church building replaced and was built over the site of a much earlier chapel of ease, which had been built in the village during the medieval period. A chapel of ease was sometimes provided during this time for communities living some distance away from their established parish church. Services, including the Sacraments, could be provided by a visiting, or resident monk, who would also, as part of his obligation to the Lord of the Manor who installed him to the position, offer daily prayers for the well-being and safety of that lord. However, Muker Chapel of Ease was established under the authority of the Vicar of Grinton and the Muker inhabitants were to pay the whole cost of the provision of a chaplain directly to the Grinton cleric, together with all fees for baptism, weddings and burials.

This arrangement, established by law, was followed for decades, until in 1750, the parishioners of Grinton successfully petitioned the church authorities to nullify the arrangement. The Elizabethan church was extremely basic. Its roof was thatched and the congregation stood or knelt on its stone floor. It was fitted with stone benches along both walls, on which the aged and infirm of the congregation sat.

This situation lasted for nearly two hundred years until, in 1761 permission was granted for the installation of a slated roof and pews to be fitted in the nave. These were allocated by lot to those of the congregation who could pay for the privilege by an additional land tax levied upon their property. The original church was fitted with a gallery and musician's platform, both of which were removed during the major restoration which took place in 1890.

The Church of St. Mary, the Virgin, Muker.

Above, Muker hay pastures and below colourful outbuildings in the village.

The Literary Institute, built in 1876, was the centre of learning for those who could read and it was stocked with around 600 books at the time. It is now 'home' to the Muker Silver Band, which was formed in 1897, as part of the celebrations of Queen Victoria's Diamond Jubilee. The band is still playing regularly and has a full engagement diary every year.

Very early settlement in the vicinity of the village has been established by the discovery in the 1950s of an early Bronze Age male skeleton, buried beneath a stone cairn at the foot of an escarpment below Arn Gill Head, opposite Kisdon and above Ivelet Wood.

The community has always been reliant on the local industries of farming, mining and knitting. The mining activities locally at Swinner Gill ceased during the late nineteenth century, after the dale's lead industry collapsed and continuous episodes of flood caused the widespread de-population of the dale. Both farming and woollen manufacturing interests continue in the village, supplemented now by intensive tourism. Population numbers in the village are steadily dwindling as more properties are sold and turned into holiday homes.

Farming activity in the area is strong, evidenced by the annual Muker Show, which attracts attendance by thousands of people each year. The show is comprehensive family fun throughout the day and includes an amazing array of activities including sheep show and handling, sheep dog trials, dog shows, games, fancy dress competition, fell races, tractor displays, competition for walking stick production and home produced foodstuffs, wine, handicrafts and wine.

The 2013 show raised a sum of £1,300, which was contributed to the Swaledale's Fell Rescue charity. Swaledale Woollens is a thriving shop in the village. It was opened by villagers more than thirty years ago to re-introduce the hand crafted woollen industry which previously existed throughout the dale as a cottage industry. Housed in an old school building is a craft shop, art gallery and café, and a tea shop is situated in what was the previous vicarage.

Ramps Holme Bridge, Muker, where the footpath from Swinnet Gill enters the village.

Footpath into Muker from Kisdon.

Above, Muker village centre and below the 'Coffin Stone'

At present, there are twelve fields at Muker growing a wide range of wild flower varieties, which each year attract many visitors, who enjoy their beauty before the harvest. There are many different species to be seen, including cat's ear, wood crane's bill, lady's mantle, pignut and the prickly thistle. These hay meadows are protected and are widely regarded as a national treasure. Wild flowers in the Yorkshire Dales became something of a rarity and are growing again thanks to years of careful management by the local farmers. The pastures are harvested every year at the end of June to provide fodder for livestock (and wild animals such as deer and rabbits) during the winter. months.

Sixteenth century packhorse bridge over the River Swale, near Ivelet.

Just over a mile and a half downstream from Muker, beside the River Swale, lies Ivelet, a tiny hamlet, where a late sixteenth century stone packhorse bridge crosses the Swale River. Beside the bridge and set into the ground is a remarkable, flat length of local stone, known as 'The Coffin Stone'.

In its position beside the bridge abutment, the stone serves no structural purpose for the bridge and is singularly out of place in its relevance to the river bank. Tradition explains its purpose as a resting place for coffins being manually carried along the Corpse Road towards Grinton for burial prior to 1580, when the opening of Muker parish churchyard dispensed with the need to carry bodies from the higher dale to Grinton for burial. Such being the case, the stone pre-dates the bridge by many years and poses a question as to what was previously here as a river crossing to create a natural resting place on the Corpse Road journey? Both stone and bridge are currently Grade 2 Listed.

Ivelet Bridge, autumn colours.

Gunnerside

The next village downstream from Muker is Gunnerside. The name is of Norse origin, (named after Gunnar, a Viking warrior) and the settlement originally consisted of two separate communities, Gunnerside to the west and Lodge Green to the east, divided by the watercourse now known as Gunnerside Beck.

The present bridge over the beck in the village was built in the 1830s, at the same time as the Gunnerside 'New Bridge', which spans the River Swale to the south of the village centre. The bridges were built at that time to alleviate hardship and unemployment in the mining industry of the period. Both bridges suffered repeated damage by the severe floods mentioned previously in the text concerning Thwaite village. The Swale river bed below the New Bridge shows clear evidence of a previous stone-laid ford, which provided an ancient river crossing at this location.

The earliest village buildings date from the seventeenth and early eighteenth centuries. Others date to the nineteenth century, and many demonstrate the prosperity brought about by lead mining by their architectural refinements such as cut sandstone door surrounds and porches. Conversion of many properties in the village into holiday cottages has taken place, with the associated reduction in permanent population.

The village, as with most of Swaledale's settlements, was largely Non-Conformist in its religious observance and at one time had two church based schools; a Methodist one, destroyed as a result of a twentieth century fire and an Anglican school (now named Gunnarsgill Hall). A Literary Institute is situated beside a small square on the village's west side. Built in 1877, it faces the village smithy, which now houses a local history museum.

Above, Gunnerside village from above Hagg Wood, with Gunnerside Gill extending into the fell towards the mine workings behind and, below, Gunnerside village square.

Above, the King's Head Inn seen from the bridge spanning Gunnerside Beck and below, Gunnerside Forge.

Since at least the beginning of the fifteenth century, lead mining was the major source of employment at Gunnerside, until the general slump in demand for the metal nationally and the commencement of import of cheaper ore from abroad in the 1870s, caused the ultimate decline of the industry. From the beginning, mining activity consisted of excavation of surface and near-surface galena deposits, but gradually these became more difficult to find. The practice of 'hushing', (creating a dam at the top of the fell and releasing huge volumes of water downhill) exposed further, workable deposits, but mining activity was eventually forced deeper and deeper, at great expense, in order to uncover workable ore.

Blakethwaite peat store and smelter ruins.

Blakethwaite Smelter ruins, Gunnerside Gill.

Quantities of galena won by the miners at Gunnerside increased sharply in 1819, to the point where improved smelting facilities were required and a new smelting mill was built at Blakethwaite in 1821. It processed ore mined at Gunnerside and had two ore-hearths fuelled with locally gathered peat and coal from Tan Hill. Fumes were drawn into a flu and chimney system extending uphill above the mill.

The 'Sir Francis Level' was a huge deposit of ore lying deep underground. It was discovered in about 1860 and the owner of the mining rights, Sir George Denys decided to commence the task of deep-mining to access the ore. The mine, named after his son, was first driven towards the deposits in 1864, and quickly began to produce quantities of the precious metal, although the mine was never to be considered as a venture of huge profit.

Tunnelling into the fells in search of the ore began as an operation of pick-axe work, hand-bored shot holes with hammer and percussion drills and highly dangerous black powder blasting. In about 1870, the mine owner, taking advantage of newly emerging mining technology, decided to improve and lessen the overall cost of the process by introducing compressed air drilling. An air compressor, driven by waterwheel; and a large steel vessel, receiving and storing compressed air, were situated in an engine house at the mouth of the level and the compressed air was piped towards the drillers by hose.

Exhaust air from the drills, despite being contaminated by lubricating oil from both the compressor and drills, and rock dust in abundance, was seen as an additional benefit to the miners, as it provided much needed extra ventilation in the workings. These (so-called) benefits enabled the men to work underground for longer periods without the need for expensive airshafts, saving further time and money in the process.

The ore dressing floor, located nearby beside the watercourse, was where lead ore was crushed, washed and sorted, before being sent to the smelting mill to be processed by furnace heat to produce molten lead. The product was then poured into moulds to produce ingots of metal. Evidence of all these activities can still be seen throughout the Gunnerside Gill area, which remains today as a devastated landscape, left behind by nineteenth century mining practice and activity.

Above, Blakethwaite peat store ruin and, pictured left, an example of a very early rivet joined, wrought iron pressure vessel, used as a compressed air receiver, that fed the pneumatic drills which Sir George Denys introduced in the Sir Francis mine, to improve operating efficiency in the 1870s.

Gunnerside Gill, Sir Francis Mines operations area

The Blakethwaite Smelting Mill began working to produce pig lead in 1821. It continued to produce lead ingots from ore produced at the Blakethwaite, Lowenthwaite and Swinnergill mines until it was closed in 1878, due to its bad state of repair and general inefficiency. Its flu originally rose from its rear to a chimney situated at the top of the escarpment, the scar of which can be clearly seen in the illustration on page 106.

In an effort to improve its overall efficiency by improved natural draught, in 1864, Sir George Denys ordered the chimney to be demolished and the flu extended by some 350 feet to a new chimney located on the moor above. After 1878, all smelting process at Gunnerside was transferred to the Surrender Mill adjacent to Barney Beck, a little distance below the Old Gang Mill.

The Blakethwaite Mill's peat supply was obtained from the moors above and sent down to be stored and dried via a wooden chute which ran parallel with the flu, some sixty metres to the west. The mill is also rather unique in having an adjacent structure, which has been described as a lime kiln, but which is more likely to be the remains of a bee-hive coking oven in which the low grade Tan Hill coal used by the process was roasted and quenched to produce furnace grade coke.

Beside the River Swale at The Strands, Gunnerside.

Low Row and Feetham

Low Row and Feetham consists of two communities in a small village settlement, situated on the sunny side of the valley, some three miles further into Swaledale from Reeth, along the B6270 road. The hamlets boast a fine, well frequented public house, named The Punchbowl Inn. The small community comprising the village is mainly extended along the dale's road, with the addition of some outlying farms.

It also has a particularly well sited and handsome Church of the Holy Trinity and a United Reformed Church. The houses of both communities are strung-out along the line of the road and are in the main sited out of site from the road, between it and the River Swale. A proportion of properties, as with most areas in the dale today, are holiday homes, so the permanent population is lower than might be expected.

At the height of the lead mining era, it was a thriving community, with men, women and children, all employed in some capacity in the lead mining and smelting trades. Most would have worked at the mines and smelters along the Hard Level Gill and Barney Beck and would have had to tramp uphill for two miles and back each day, to earn a crust or two in what was very hard labour. The valley floor at this point is very narrow, with extremely steep sides, so very little arable, easily worked, productive land was available for miner or farmer. Feeding hard working families was problematical all year round, but was especially so in the winter months.

Although there is no village actually called Melbecks, (meaning Middle Beck in Norse), the name seems to have become permanently attached to the little, simple English style church in Low Row. One of only four Anglican churches in Swaledale, building work on the Church of the Holy Trinity commenced in 1814 and was completed the same year, when the church was consecrated as a chapel to the main church at Grinton.

Pages 112 and 113 author's painting of Low Row and Feetham.

Above, the Punch Bowl Inn, Low Row, and below, 'Melbecks' Church.

Above, Low Row bridge over the River Swale and, below, cottages on the B6270 at Low Row.

This page images, the Surrender Smeling Mill and peat store beside Barney Beck.

There could not possibly be a more open, totally exposed place in which to work, than Reeth High and Low Moors, where the Old Gang and Surrender smelting mills are situated.

In 1806, the Surrender Mill was built to replace two much older smelting mills on the site and the stonework of those mills was re-used in the new building work. The mill produced lead ingots in quantity and smelted much of Gunnerside's Sir Francis Mine's output of ore, as well as output from the more local mines, until the beginning of the industry's decline in the 1870s.

Production ceased altogether in 1880 and finally, the site was sold in 1902, when everything of use, or value was dismantled and taken away. Since then the site has been listed as an important Ancient Monument, and is accordingly protected by law.

Looking carefully at this and other similar sites, one has to marvel at the ingenuity of the industrial stone masons and builders of the period, in their use of local rough stone in the working structures, whether rubble, dressed stone, or worked slab. Given that the structures stood working for 70 years, exposed openly to the roughest of elements and purposely subjected to the harshest temperature changes possible, the surviving buildings demonstrate the cleverness of design and the skill of raising them from the turf.

A high proportion of the population, young and old, of Low Row, Feetham and Healaugh would have toiled here daily to work in the mills or adjacent mines throughout the year, in all weathers; carrying with them what food and drink they required to see them through the long days of work.

Surrender Mill with twin flue arrangement towards the chimney.

Barney Beck and Surrender Bridge.

The western end of Healaugh.

Healaugh

The village of Healaugh lies on the B6270 road about a mile from Reeth. Facing south, one looks across the River Swale to Harkerside Fell and the white rock scar of the crags of High Harker Hill, just below which lies the Iron Age earthworks of Maiden Castle. The area of the village and its immediate surroundings has been settled by people since the Bronze Age and records date from as early as Domesday.

Today however, the population has fallen and many of the houses in the village have become holiday homes; in years past, villagers were heavily involved with mining, farming and the woollen trade. The main occupation of the present permanent residents of the village (those who are not commuting daily to the towns of Richmond or Darlington, or elsewhere), is farming.

The layout of the village follows the line of the main road running through it. The cottages present a pretty aspect, being stone built, with stone or slate roofs. The red telephone box, situated beside the centre square, is famous for its sumptuous appointments as a village amenity, fitted out with carpet, waste bin, fresh flowers, books and a little box for donations.

The Coast to Coast long distance walking route passes the village a few hundred yards away on its northern side and it has cross fell road connections, north and south, to Arkengarthdale and Wensleydale

Above, the village square and famous telephone box and, below looking south east towards the suspension foobridge over the River Swale

Images on this page, Healaugh cottage garden, cottages and a farmyard.

Swaledale from Kearton.

Reeth

Well situated on the B6270 road, some twelve miles west of Richmond, Reeth lies just to the north of the River Swale, at the southern end of Arkengarthdale, where it joins Swaledale, and the Arkle Beck joins the River Swale.

The settlement of Reeth is an ancient possibly Celtic settlement which had existed on its plateau above the Swale for some centuries. Reeth grew with the arrival of Vikings, Saxons and Normans and was of sufficient importance to be mentioned in the Domesday book. The village layout has Saxon influence with its typical arrangement of dwellings grouped around a central grassed area, where livestock could be brought to complete safety in times of external threat.

After 1066 Norman inspired defensive and ecclesiastical building programmes throughout Britain blossomed. This caused an immediate and on-going demand for lead as an easy to work, malleable material, used to weatherproof roofs and to create strong metal-to-stone joints within the structures being built, as well as its use to line water conduits. Demand for British lead also came from the Norman homeland, as throughout Normandy and France, large cathedral and church building programmes took shape.

A widespread, increasing demand for lead, at home and abroad, continued over the next five centuries, as populations of Britain and Europe increased and stabilised, creating further, general building programmes. Richmond and Reeth were ideally placed to become administrative centres for the collection and onward distribution of this valuable product, plentifully available from the two dales.

Subsequently, Reeth began to gain importance as a source of support for the lead producing industry of the two dales. More lead demand brought about population increases along the dales and increased population naturally meant more demand for food and accommodation.

These influences created a huge growth of supporting tradesmen: carpenters, masons, tin and lead smiths, bakers, brewers, carters, smiths and farriers, most of which naturally centred themselves upon the conveniently situated Reeth as a base.

Above, late spring snow above Reeth and, below, the east side of the village green

Above, Reeth from Grinton Lodge and below the Buck Inn and road to Arkengarthdale.

The woollen industry and hand knitting activity in the dales also grew from Elizabethan times and Reeth became an organising centre for this important industry. The knitting was mostly of stockings and was carried out by men, women and children.

The Swaledale and Arkengarthdale lead industry grew in prominence and output and peaked by about the 1850s. Thereafter, it commenced a dramatic downward trend, which was heavily influenced by cheap imported metal and the dire hardship created for the dales folk (miner, tradesman and farmer alike), by the terrible and catastrophic, periodic weather episodes of the nineteenth century.

Above, the Black Bull Hotel and terrace facing the village green, below, Reeth Congregational Church.

As the people of upper Swaledale and Arkengarthdale, meeting hard times, became more and more destitute, Reeth Poorhouse, built in Back Lane in 1753, became full to capacity. With no respite or support, people began to move away from every settlement, including Reeth, many moving to the more southern counties, but more still, emigrating to America, or Spain. Notwithstanding this massive reduction in population the village of Reeth managed to retain its importance in support of the remaining Swaledale and Arkengarthdale communities.

Modern Reeth still has houses, two fine pubs and shops clustered around the triangular, sloping village green. It has a magnificent Congregational Church, a thriving art community, galleries and cafés, a museum and a regular Friday market. Additionally, and very importantly, each year it hosts the Swaledale Festival and the Reeth Show. It has become an important centre for tourism in the two dales and a resting point for Coast to Coast walkers on their treks in either direction across the country.

The Copper Kettle and the south east approach road to the village green, Reeth.

Above, the Fat Sheep and Old Temperance Bookshop, and below Reeth School,

Above, Anvil Square, and below, the Arkle Beck road bridge near Reeth.

12
Arkengarthdale: The Villages

A dis-similar twin to Swaledale, Arkengarthdale commences at Reeth and extends north west for some ten miles to its summit on Sleightholm Moor. The road along the dale eventually reaches the Tan Hill Inn, where it joins the road rising through Stonesdale from Keld and the road from Stainmore into Cumbria. Its geography makes it the northernmost dale in the North Yorkshire National Park.

The Arkle Beck rises from its summit and flows down through the dale, to meet the River Swale between Reeth and Grinton. Several small tributary watercourses join it as it traverses down the dale, passing settlements of varying size such as: Whaw, Eskeleth, Langthwaite (the only settlement of any significant size remaining in the dale), Arkle Town (which ceased to be anything like a town in size decades ago), and finally Raw. A hamlet named Booze lies about a mile east of Langthwaite, towards the once very active lead mining site on both sides of Slei Gill. Many names in the dale are testament to a Norse heritage and the name Arkengarthdale is thought to derive from a Viking chieftain named Arkil.

Arkengarthdale has long been synonymous with lead mining and evidence suggests that the Romans were operating mines with slave labour in the dale as early as the first decades of the second century. The Norse names and the typical scattered upland settlements in the dale, suggest that the area was settled by Norsemen arriving from the west in the tenth century.

After 1066 William the Conquerer's nephew, Alain le Roux selected Arkengarthdale and its adjacent forests as his personal hunting domain. Local people were thereafter prevented from carrying out any form of game hunting by ever present gamekeepers. In Alain le Roux's time the game wardens did not flinch from exacting the ultimate form of punishment on anyone caught with a bow or spear within his land. The area was proscribed and managed as a game reserve for the following four centuries, although some farming of land was permitted and tenants of the lord were allowed to build their own houses.

The Earls of Richmond died out by the late 1500s and at that time the land, with a recorded 55 farming tenants, reverted to the Crown. On 11 May 1625, Charles I married Henrietta Maria of France. Despite his agreement to provide the French with English ships as a condition of marrying Henrietta Maria, in 1627 the English king launched an attack on the French coast to defend the Huguenots at La Rochelle. The King's finances were to say the least, sorely pressed to fund these huge expenses, and in the attempts to realise funds from his existing assets, among many other similar areas, Arkengarthdale was sold to the City of London.

The estate was eventually sold again in 1656, and passed to Oliver Cromwell's doctor, Charles Bathurst. It remained in the Bathurst family until 1740, when, subject to inheritance by three sisters, it was divided into three separate parts. The three parcels of land came together again by 1811, after being purchased by a banker.

Arkengarthdale has featured in popular television series, such as, *All Creatures Great and Small,* and *A Woman of Substance*.

Booze

The hillside on which the hamlet of Booze sits, contained many lead mining levels. Always a dangerous occupation, the mine tunnels around Slei Gill had perhaps more than their fair share of catastrophe. In the eighteenth century a group of miners working underground near Boldershaw blasted into an underground lake drowning 24 miners and two pit ponies in the flood that followed, eighteen of the dead miners came from Booze.

The vein of ore being followed, thereafter became known as the Water Blast Vein. After the decline of the lead mining industry in North Yorkshire at the end of the nineteenth century, one of the mines, the Booze Wood Level, continued to be used as a slate mine until the beginning of the First World War.

Booze hamlet

In July 2008 Royal Mail withdrew postal services from Booze on health and safety grounds due to the excessively steep and narrow rural track leading to the hamlet. Mail deliveries were only resumed after North Yorkshire County Council made road improvements.

The whole area of fells and crags bounding the lower and middle sections of Arkengarthdale is riddled with the remains of eighteenth and nineteenth century lead mining activity. None more so than Fremington Edge, which is a three miles long wall of steep scree slopes and verticle crags situated between Hurst and Marrick Moors and the Arkle Beck, immediately to the north of Reeth.

Chert was mined on Fremington Edge until the beginning of the Second World War. Chert is a microcrystalline or cryptocrystalline sedimentary rock material composed of silicon dioxide ($SiO2$). It occurs as nodules, concretionary masses, and as layered deposits. When chert breaks it often produces very sharp edges which is why it was used by Late Mesolithic and Early Neolithic people to fashion cutting tools and weapons. The name 'flint' is also used for this material, although chert cannot be knapped as predictably as true flint.

Above Langthwaite and below, the Charles Bathurst Inn.

Langthwaite

Langthwaite is the main settlement in the dale. It lies around the main turnpike road through the dale, which was opened in 1770, improving the means and speed of transporting lead and other goods within and out of the dale. It has a fine church, consecrated to St Mary the Virgin, which is known as a Commissioner's Church.

A Commissioner's church is an Anglican church built with money voted by Parliament as a result of the Church Building Act of 1818 and 1824. They have been given a number of titles, including Commissioners churches, Waterloo churches and Million Act churches. The Commission was founded on a wave of national triumph following the defeat of Napoleon at the Battle of Waterloo in 1815; hence the suggestion of the word 'Waterloo' in the title.

The Church of St Mary the Virgin, Langthwaite.

Scar House, which sits on a hillside above the village, surrounded by trees, is an imposing residence with an interesting history. It is believed to have been built by the Gilpin Brown family, eventual heirs of the Bathhurst family who financed the renovation of the church and the building of the local school.

The later succession of residents of Scar House, include Colonel Guy Greville Wilson, who was a close friend of Edward VII, when he was Prince of Wales. The colonel was forced to sell the house to meet his gambling debts and Sir Thomas Sopwith (of First World War fighter plane fame) bought it. His wife, Lady Sopwith took offence at the higher location of another local grand residence, called Eskeleth Hall. Her disapproval led eventually to its being demolished.

In a field at Langthwaite, well away from any other dwelling, but very easily seen from the road, sits an isolated octagonal, stone building. It was built in 1807, to house the gunpowder used for blasting in the local lead mining operations. It was also in everyday use, when eventually black powder was replaced by dynamite.

Above the octagonal explosives store and below Scar House, Langthwaite

Arkle Town

As mentioned above, Arkle Town is by no means a town, but a very small hamlet whose population must have been greater in times past. Arkle Town did have a small church and a poor house. In 1812, the church was considered to be too small for the needs of the community, and was also in imminent danger of being undermined by the Arkle Beck. Consequently, the church was demolished and was re-placed by the Church of St Mary the Virgin, further up the dale in Langthwaite. A few grave stones still mark the site where the church once stood.

Grazing cattle beside the approach road to Grinton. The Lodge can be seen on the hillside above.

Grinton

The village of Grinton is situated on the southern bank of the River Swale, about one mile south east of Reeth, at a point where the relatively open, fertile lower dale changes its character, to become the wilder, more rugged, narrowed dale of the upland area.

As a settlement, it has existed since at least the early Iron Age period and became the parish centre of Swaledale up to and including Keld. The parish Church of St Andrew is located facing the main 'T' junction in the village. Its churchyard was the final destination for centuries, of those unfortunate people carrying deceased friends or relatives along the Corpse Road for burial, until the few other churchyards were established further up the dale.

Offering proof of the age of the Grinton settlement as a whole, Iron Age earthworks can be seen sited between the river and the village below the bridge on two knolls of glacial morain, which have been left by a retreating glacier. The bridge dates from the fifteenth century and spans the river above what was the first available sensible fording place beyond Richmond.

Half a mile above Grinton, on the road towards Cogden Moor, lies Grinton Lodge, a nineteenth century shooting lodge, which, since 1948, has been used as a youth hostel. Travelling upwards for about another mile, one arrives at the Grinton lead mining area and smelter ruins on Grinton Moor.

Above Grinton village seen from the B6270 and below St. Andrew's Parish Church, Grinton.

The interior of St. Andrew's Church, showing the font, nave and an extraordinary escutcheon, below.

The Norman origin of St Andrew's Church can be seen from the character of the impressive tower. It underwent alterations to its size three times in three successive centuries, from the fourteenth century onwards. However, in the late nineteenth century, the church was found to be too small and in a bad state of repair. During a period of six years, the building was completely renovated and enlarged and was re-opened for worship in 1896.

The escutcheon hanging above the chancel steps is of particular interest. Normally, the reverse side coat of arms facing the priest and altar is that of the Diocesan Bishop, to whom the priest has allegiance and responsibility, while the side facing the congregation shows the Royal Coat of Arms. In the case of Grinton Church, both sides display the Royal emblem, as the church traditionally has always been in the Gift of the King; and the officiating priest has allegiance to the Monarch.

The Bridge Inn opposite the church, was a coaching inn. It dates from the fifteenth century and is notable today for its welcoming hospitality, (especially towards dogs and muddy boots) and the resident Swaledale sheep standing on its roof!

Above, the Bridge Inn, Grinton and below the village viewed from the new cemetery.

The bridge crossing and River Swale at Grinton.

Swaledale from Marrick Moor

Lower Swaledale from Whitecliffe Scar

River Swale and Hudswell from Whitecliffe Scar

Richmond from approach to Whitecliffe Wood.

So we have come in a full circle of discovery within what I consider to be one of the loveliest of landscapes in the British Isles. I do not claim that the Swaledale area is the best or the most interesting of areas in these isles, but it is undoubtedly beautiful and still rather wild; full of interest and spectacle and its local people are truly the salt of the earth.

I have not covered every nook and cranny, every hamlet or community; there is much to see that is not described here and much left to learn about the people of these dales living among its varied fells and hollows. I hope that I have described and shown to the reader of this rather humble book of mine, sufficient to raise his/her interest and curiosity, and enough to promote their interest sufficiently for them to need to visit the area for themselves and experience for themselves what they cannot see, touch, hear or smell from this book. I can honestly say that they will not be disappointed.

Peter Moppett, Summer 2017

Peter Moppett was an Electrical Engineer for most of his working life, starting as a research assistant, working on radar pulse development and wind tunnel design, before experiencing a little over two years as a rather elderly, four years deferred, National Serviceman, serving with the Royal Corps of Signals. During which time, he met, Mary, his wife of 55 years.

Continuing his career after Army service, he specialised in the design of power distribution and control systems for ferrous and non-ferrous metallurgical smelting plants, which took him to several different countries, before settling into a totally different career as a senior Local Government Officer.

Peter has always shown a passion for photography and landscape art and since retirement to North Yorkshire has developed some skill as a digital painter, activities which he has combined in the production of this book.